A FRAMEWORK FOR

UNDERSTANDING POVERTY

FOURTH REVISED EDITION

A FRAMEWORK FOR
UNDERSTANDING POVERTY

FOURTH REVISED EDITION

Ruby K. Payne, Ph.D.

aha!
Process, Inc.

A Framework for Understanding Poverty. Fourth revised edition.
© 1996 by aha! Process, Inc. Revised 1998, 2001, 2003, 2005.

aha! Process, Inc.
P.O. Box 727
Highlands, TX 77562-0727
(800) 424-9484 ■ (281) 426-5300
Fax: (281) 426-5600
Website: www.ahaprocess.com

Book design by Sara Patton
Printed in the United States of America

Payne, Ruby K.
    A Framework for Understanding Poverty. Fourth revised
        edition.
    Ruby K. Payne 1996. 216 pp.
        Bibliography pp. 187–193
        ISBN 13: 978-1-929229-48-2
        ISBN 10: 1-929229-48-8
    1. Education   2. Sociology   3. Title

Contents

OTHER SELECTED TITLES BY RUBY K. PAYNE, PH.D.

Un Marco Para Entender La Pobreza (Spanish translation of *Framework*)

Understanding Learning

Learning Structures

Preventing School Violence by Creating Emotional Safety:
Video Series & Manual

*Meeting Standards & Raising Test Scores—When You Don't Have
Much Time or Money: Video Series & Manual* (Payne & Magee)

Removing the Mask: Giftedness in Poverty (Slocumb & Payne)

Bridges Out of Poverty: Strategies for Professionals and Communities
(Payne, DeVol, & Dreussi Smith)

Think Rather of Zebra (Stailey & Payne)

What Every Church Member Should Know About Poverty (Payne & Ehlig)

Living on a Tightrope—A Survival Handbook for Principals
(Sommers & Payne)

Hidden Rules of Class at Work (Payne & Krabill)

Acknowledgments

A very special thanks to . . .

Judy Duncan, the assistant principal at Bowie Elementary School, who first approached me with the idea of writing a book about poverty.

The teachers at Bowie Elementary, who were so gracious and receptive to the ideas presented to them.

Sara Hector, field service agent for the Texas Education Agency, whose continuing encouragement and support led to the development of this book.

Jay Stailey, principal at Carver Elementary School and president of the National Storytelling Association, whose conversations about poverty and stories stimulated my thinking.

Karen Coffey, colleague and Project Read consultant, who provided suggestions.

Carol Ellis, my secretary, who knew the hours I was putting in at home on the book and was supportive.

Sue Franta, for all her assistance and support.

Cheryl Evans, for her illustrations, editing, and layout design.

Jim Grant and Dan Shenk, for their editing assistance.

Donna Magee, for her assistance with the Research Notes.

Anna Elmore, for her countless revisions and endless patience.

The TEAM project members at the University of Houston-Clear Lake for their interest and encouragement.

Frank Payne, my former husband, and Tom Payne, our son, whose patience, support, encouragement, and love have allowed this book to happen.

aha! Process, Inc. exists to improve the education and lives of individuals in poverty around the world. It provides an additive model that recognizes that people in poverty, middle class, and wealth are all problem solvers. The focus is on solutions, shared responsibilities, new insights, and inter-dependence. This work is about the resulting connectedness and about relationships; it is about "us."

Additive Model: aha! Process's Approach to Building High-Achieving Schools

SUMMARY

An *additive model*, implicit throughout this book and analyzed more directly in the Appendix on page 163, is a vital tool for better understanding and addressing poverty, as well as the underlying factors that perpetuate it.

Dr. Ruby K. Payne's additive model:

■ Honors internal assets of people from all economic classes.

■ Names problems accurately.

■ Identifies the mindsets and patterns that individuals use to survive different economic environments—and provides a vocabulary to talk about it.

■ Identifies strengths and resources already found in the individual, family, school, and community—and adds new information and a new perspective for creating and growing resources.

■ Offers economic diversity as a prism through which individuals and schools can analyze and respond to their issues.

■ Identifies skills, theories of change, program designs, partnerships, and ways of building schools where students achieve.

■ Encourages the development of strategies to respond to all causes of poverty.

Introduction

This book came to be because so many people were asking questions that, finally, I promised to put things in writing. My name is Ruby Payne, and I never realized that the information I had gathered over the years about poverty, middle class, and wealth would be of interest to other people.

It wasn't until an assistant principal, Judy Duncan, came to me and asked about a staff-development program for her faculty on discipline—and referenced the number of student referrals they were having—that I even began talking about the differences. She noted how the population in the school had changed over the past three years from 24% low income (as measured by the number of students on free and reduced-price lunch) to 60% low income. As she described the kinds of discipline situations they were experiencing, I would explain why those behaviors were happening. Finally, she stopped me and asked where I was getting my information. It was at that point that I realized that I had been gathering data for 24 years.

Where had I gotten the data? First of all, I was married more than 30 years to Frank, who grew up in poverty because his father died when he was 6. Though it was situational poverty, he lived for several years with those who were in generational poverty. Over the years, as I met his family and the many other players in the "neighborhood," I came to realize there were major differences between generational poverty and middle class—and that the biggest differences were not about money. But what put the whole picture into bas-relief were the six years we spent in Illinois among the wealthy. It was the addition of the third dimension, wealth, that clarified the differences between and among poverty, middle class, and wealth.

As the principal of an affluent elementary school in Illinois, I began to rethink so much of what I had thought about poverty and wealth. The Illinois students had no more native intelligence than the poor students I had worked with earlier in my career. And I noticed that the achievement levels of affluent African-American, Hispanic, and Asian children were no different from those of affluent Caucasian children.

So, at Judy Duncan's request, I shared the information with her faculty members. They were very interested and thought the information was helpful. One teacher told another, and soon I was doing several workshops in other districts. Sara Hector, a field service agent with the Texas Education Agency, attended a workshop and told many people about it. Then Jay Stailey, another principal, asked me to come with him to the University of Houston-Clear Lake to meet with a grant consortium, of which he was co-chair. This session led to more meetings and conversations.

So this information has spread more quickly than I could have ever anticipated. I just hope this data will be helpful to you, the reader, as well.

SOME KEY POINTS TO REMEMBER

1. *Poverty is relative.* If everyone around you has similar circumstances, the notion of poverty and wealth is vague. Poverty or wealth only exists in relationship to known quantities or expectations.

2. *Poverty occurs in all races and in all countries.* The notion of middle class as a large segment of society is a phenomenon of this century. The percentage of the population that is poor is subject to definition and circumstance.

3. *Economic class is a continuous line, not a clear-cut distinction.* In 2006, the poverty line in the United States was considered $20,444 for a family of four. According to census data from 2006, the median household income was $48,451 and 19% of U.S. households earned more than $100,000 per year. Individuals are stationed all along the continuum of income; they sometimes move on that continuum as well.

4. *Generational poverty and situational poverty are different.* Generational poverty is defined as being in poverty for two generations or longer. Situational poverty is a shorter time and is caused by circumstance (i.e., death, illness, divorce, etc.).

5. *This work is based on patterns. All patterns have exceptions.*

6. *An individual brings with him/her the hidden rules of the class in which he/she was raised.* Even though the income of the individual may rise significantly, many of the patterns of thought, social interaction, cognitive strategies, etc., remain with the individual.

7. *Schools and businesses operate from middle-class norms and use the hidden rules of middle class.* These norms and hidden rules are not directly taught in schools or in businesses.

8. *For our students to be successful, we must understand their hidden rules and teach them the rules that will make them successful at school and at work.*

9. *We can neither excuse students nor scold them for not knowing; as educators we must teach them and provide support, insistence, and expectations.*

10. *To move from poverty to middle class or middle class to wealth, an individual must give up relationships for achievement (at least for some period of time).*

11. *Two things that help one move out of poverty are education and relationships.*

12. *Four reasons one leaves poverty are: It's too painful to stay, a vision or goal, a key relationship, or a special talent or skill.*

SOME STATISTICS ABOUT POVERTY

1. In the United States in 2006, the poverty rate for all individuals was 12.3%. For children under the age of 18, the poverty rate was 17.4%, and for children under the age of 5, the rate was 20.4%. (U.S. Census Bureau, 2007).

2. There were 7.7 million poor families (9.8%) in 2006, up from 6.4 million (6.7%) in 2000 (U.S. Census Bureau, 2007).

3. The foreign-born population in the United States has increased 57% since 1990 to a total of 30 million. In 2000, one out of every five children under age 18 in the U.S. was estimated to have at least one foreign-born parent. Immigrant children are twice as likely to be poor as native-born children. Among children whose parents work full time, immigrant children are at greater risk of living in poverty than native-born children (National Center for Children in Poverty, Columbia University, 2002).

4. Regardless of race or ethnicity, poor children are much more likely than non-poor children to suffer developmental delay and damage, to drop out of high school, and to give birth during the teen years (Miranda, 1991).

5. Poverty-prone children are more likely to be in single-parent families (Einbinder, 1993). Median female wages in the United States, at all levels of educational attainment, are 30 to 50% lower than male wages at the same level of educational attainment (TSII Manual, 1995, based on U.S. Census data, 1993). See 2006 U.S. census data on page 115.

6. Poor inner-city youths are seven times more likely to be the victims of child abuse or neglect than are children of high social and economic status (Renchler, 1993).

7. Poverty is caused by interrelated factors: parental employment status and earnings, family structure, and parental education (Five Million Children, 1992).

8. Children under age 5 remain particularly vulnerable to poverty. In 2006 children under 5 living in families with a female householder and no husband present experienced a poverty rate of 53.7%, more than five times the rate for children in married-couple families, 9.6% (U.S. Census Bureau, 2007).

9. The United States' child poverty rate is substantially higher — often two or three times higher — than that of most other major Western industrialized nations.

10. In the 2006, the following racial percentages and numbers of poor children were reported.

United States	Number of Children in Poverty in 2006	Percentage of Children in Poverty
All Races	12,896,000	17.6%
Caucasian	7,908,000	14.1%
Hispanic*	4,072,000	26.9%
African-American	3,777,000	33.4%
Asian-American	360,000	12.2%
Native American **	194,272	31.9%

* Hispanics may be of any race.

** Native American numbers from 2000 Decennial Census (not counted in 2006).

Source: U.S. Census Bureau and Bureau of Labor Statistics, *2007 Annual Demographic Survey*

NOTE: The U.S. Census Bureau publishes income and poverty data each year for the previous calendar year. For the most current information provided in this format, visit www.ahaprocess.com.

11. While the number of Caucasian children in poverty is the largest group, the percentage of children in poverty in most minority groups is higher.

CHAPTER 1

Definitions and Resources

To better understand students and adults from poverty, a working definition of poverty is "the extent to which an individual does without resources." These resources are the following:

FINANCIAL: Having the money to purchase goods and services.

EMOTIONAL: Being able to choose and control emotional responses, particularly to negative situations, without engaging in self-destructive behavior. This is an internal resource and shows itself through stamina, perseverance, and choices.

MENTAL: Having the mental abilities and acquired skills (reading, writing, computing) to deal with daily life.

SPIRITUAL: Believing in divine purpose and guidance.

PHYSICAL: Having physical health and mobility.

SUPPORT SYSTEMS: Having friends, family, and backup resources available to access in times of need. These are external resources.

RELATIONSHIPS/ROLE MODELS: Having frequent access to adult(s) who are appropriate, who are *nurturing* to the child, and who do not engage in self-destructive behavior.

KNOWLEDGE OF HIDDEN RULES: Knowing the unspoken cues and habits of a group.

Typically, poverty is thought of in terms of financial resources only. However, the reality is that *financial resources*, while extremely important, do not explain the differences in the success with which individuals leave poverty nor the reasons that many stay in poverty. The ability to leave poverty is more dependent upon other resources than it is upon financial resources. Each of these resources plays a vital role in the success of an individual.

Emotional resources provide the stamina to withstand difficult and uncomfortable emotional situations and feelings. Emotional resources are the most important of all resources because, when present, they allow the individual not to return to old habit patterns. In order to move from poverty to middle class or middle class to wealth, an individual must suspend his/her "emotional memory bank" because the situations and hidden rules are so unlike what he/she has experienced previously. Therefore, a certain level of persistence and an ability to stay with the situation until it can be learned (and therefore feel comfortable) are necessary. This persistence (i.e., staying with the situation) is proof that emotional resources are present. Emotional resources come, at least in part, from role models.

Mental resources are simply being able to process information and use it in daily living. If an individual can read, write, and compute, he/she has a decided advantage. That person can access information from many different free sources, as well as be somewhat self-sufficient.

Spiritual resources are the belief that help can be obtained from a higher power, that there is a purpose for living, and that worth and love are gifts from God. This is a powerful resource because the individual does not see him/herself as hopeless and useless, but rather as capable and having worth and value.

Physical resources are having a body that works, that is capable and mobile. The individual can be self-sufficient.

Support systems are resources. To whom does one go when help is needed? Those individuals available and who will help are resources. When the child is sick and you have to be at work—who takes care of the child? Where do you go when money is short and the baby needs medicine? Support systems are not just about meeting financial or emotional needs.

They are about knowledge bases as well. How do you get into college? Who sits and listens when you get rejected? Who helps you negotiate the mountains of paper? Who assists you with your algebra homework when you don't know how to do it? Those people are all support systems.

Relationships/role models are resources. All individuals have role models. The question is the extent to which the role model is nurturing or appropriate. Can the role model parent? Work successfully? Provide a gender role for the individual? It is largely from role models that the person learns how to live life emotionally.

> *No significant learning occurs*
> *without a significant relationship.*
>
> – Dr. James Comer

Knowledge of hidden rules is crucial to whatever class in which the individual wishes to live. Hidden rules exist in poverty, in middle class, and in wealth, as well as in ethnic groups and other units of people. Hidden rules are about the salient, unspoken understandings that cue the members of the group that this individual does or does not fit. For example, three of the hidden rules in poverty are the following: The noise level is high (the TV is always on and everyone may talk at once), the most important information is non-verbal, and one of the main values of an individual to the group is an ability to entertain. There are hidden rules about food, dress, decorum, etc. Generally, in order to successfully move from one class to the next, it is important to have a spouse or mentor from the class to which you wish to move to model and teach you the hidden rules.

SCENARIOS

These scenarios have been written to portray the cases with which I have become acquainted. These scenarios have deliberately omitted most of the physical, sexual, and emotional abuse that can be present so that the discussion can be about resources.

After each scenario, identify the resources available to the child and those available to the adult.

SCENARIO #1: JOHN AND ADELE
Background

John is an 8-year-old Caucasian boy. His father is a doctor and remarried but does not see his children. He pays minimal child support. The mother, Adele, works part time and is an alcoholic. One younger sibling, a girl who is mentally and physically handicapped, lives with the mother and John.

You are Adele, John's mother. You are a 29-year-old female. You quit college your sophomore year so that you could go to work to support John's father as he went through medical school. You were both elated when John was born. During the time your husband was an intern, you found that a drink or two or three in the evening calmed you down, especially since your husband was gone so much. When your second child was born, she was severely handicapped. Both of you were in shock. A year later your husband finished his residency, announced that he was in love with another woman, and divorced you. Last you heard, your husband is driving a Porsche, and he and his new wife spent their most recent vacation in Cancún. Your parents are dead. You have a sister who lives 50 miles away. Your weekly income, including child support, is $300 before taxes. Your handicapped child is 3 years old and is in day care provided by the school district.

Current Situation

You have been late to work for the third time this month. Your car broke down, and it will take $400 to fix it. Your boss told you that you will be docked a day's pay—and that if you're late again, you will be fired. You don't know how you're going to get to work tomorrow. You consider several choices: (1) You can go car shopping, (2) you can put the car in the garage and worry about the money later, (3) you can invite the mechanic over for dinner, (4) you can get mad and quit, (5) you can call your ex and threaten to take him back to court unless he pays for the car, (6) you can get a second job, or (7) you can get drunk.

Your daughter has had another seizure, and you took her to the doctor (one of the reasons you were late for work). The new medicine will cost you $45 every month.

John comes home from school and announces that the school is going to have a reading contest. Every book you read with him will earn points for him. Each book is one point, and he wants to earn 100 points. You must do physical therapy with your daughter each evening for 30 minutes, as well as get dinner. For John to get his books, he needs you to go to the library with him. You have only enough gas to go to work and back for the rest of the week, maybe not that. He also tells you that the school is having an open house, and he will get a pencil if you come. But John is not old enough to watch your daughter. Your ex has already threatened to bring up in court that you are an unfit mother if you try to get more money from him.

The mechanic calls and invites you out to dinner. He tells you that you might be able to work something out in terms of payment. It has been a long time since you have been out, and he is good-looking and seems like a nice man.

What are Adele and John's resources? Check yes by the resources that are present, check no by the ones that are not, or check question mark where the resources are uncertain.

RESOURCES — SCENARIO #1	YES	NO	?
Financial			
Emotional			
Mental			
Spiritual			
Physical			
Support systems			
Knowledge of middle-class hidden rules			
Role models			

SCENARIO #2: OTIS AND VANGIE

Background

Otis is a 9-year-old African-American boy. His mother conceived him at 14, dropped out of school, and is on welfare. Otis has two younger siblings and one older sibling who is a gang member.

You are Otis's mother, Vangie. You are a 24-year-old female. You were the oldest of five children. You had your first child when you were 13. You have received welfare and food stamps since the birth of your first child. You lived with your mother until your fourth child was born when you were 18. Then you got your own place. You dropped out of school when you were pregnant with Otis. School was always difficult for you, and you never did feel comfortable reading much anyway. Your current boyfriend comes often and he works sometimes. Your mother lives down the street. Your weekly income (including food stamps) is $215. You move a lot because there are always more bills at the end of the month than money.

Current Situation

Your sister calls and tells you that her boyfriend has beaten her again, and she needs to come spend the night at your house. The last time she came she stayed for two weeks, and her 12-year-old handicapped son would not leave your 5-year-old daughter alone. You have several choices: (1) You could take her in and make her pay for her meals, (2) you could not take her in and have the whole family mad at you, (3) you could tell your daughter to hit her cousin when he comes close, (4) you could make Otis take care of the handicapped son, (5) you could slap the fool out of the handicapped son, (6) you could use the rent money to pay for the extra food, (7) you could go partying together and let Otis take care of the kids, or (8) you could move to a bigger place.

Otis comes home from school and announces that the school is going to have a reading contest. For every five books you read to him, he will receive a coupon to get $2 off a pizza. To obtain his books, he needs you to go to the library. Also, you aren't sure you can even read to him because your skills were never good, and you haven't read for a long time. Getting to the library requires that you walk because you don't have a car. There have been two drive-by shootings last week. He also tells you that the school is having an open house and is sending a bus around the neighborhood to pick up parents. He gives you a note that you can't read.

You are probably going to have to move again. This week Otis got cut badly at school, and the school nurse took him to the emergency room; they want $200. Rent is due for the month, and it's $300 for three bedrooms. Sister is coming, and that means extra food because she never has any money. Your boyfriend got arrested and wants you to get him out of jail. He was arrested for assault. The bondsman wants $500. Your ex-boyfriend knew better than to come around. You need your boyfriend because his money makes it possible to keep from going hungry.

The teacher calls and tells you that Otis is misbehaving again. You beat the fool out of him with a belt and tell him he better behave. But that night you fix him his favorite dinner, then you tell everyone you talk to how Otis is misbehaving and what a burden he is to you.

What are Otis and Vangie's resources? Check yes by the resources that are present, check no by the ones that are not, or check question mark where the resources are uncertain.

RESOURCES — SCENARIO #2	YES	NO	?
Financial			
Emotional			
Mental			
Spiritual			
Physical			
Support systems			
Knowledge of middle-class hidden rules			
Role models			

SCENARIO #3: OPIE AND OPRAH

Background

Opie is a 12-year-old African-American girl and the oldest of five children. She runs the household because her mother, Oprah, works long hours as a domestic. Grandmother, who is 80, is senile and lives with them, as well as an out-of-work uncle.

You are Opie's mother, Oprah. You are a 32-year-old female. You were married for 10 years to your husband, and then he was killed in a car accident on the way to work two years ago. You work long hours as a domestic for a doctor. You go to the Missionary Baptist Church every Sunday where you lead the choir. Your employer treats you well and you take home about $300 every week. You ride public transportation to work and the church bus on Sunday. You want your children to go to college, even though you only finished high school.

Current Situation

Your employer gives you a $400 Christmas bonus. You thank the Lord at church for the gift. After church, three different people approach you privately. One asks for $50 to have the electricity turned on; one asks for $100 to feed her brother's family; one asks for $60 to replace a pair of broken glasses. You were hoping to save some money for an emergency.

Opie has the opportunity to be in a state-sponsored competition that requires after-school practices. You want her to do that, but you must have her at home after school every day.

What resources do Opie and Oprah have? Check yes by the resources that are present, check no by the ones that are not, or check question mark where the resources are uncertain.

RESOURCES — SCENARIO #3	YES	NO	?
Financial			
Emotional			
Mental			
Spiritual			
Physical			
Support systems			
Knowledge of middle-class hidden rules			
Role models			

SCENARIO #4: MARIA AND NOEMI

Background

Maria is a 10-year-old Hispanic girl. Her mother does not drive or speak English. Father speaks some English. Maria is a second-generation Hispanic born in the United States. Mother does not work outside the home. Father works for minimum wage as a concrete worker. There are five children. The family gets food stamps, and the mother is a devout Catholic.

You are Maria's mother, Noemi. You are a 27-year-old Hispanic female. You have five children. You have been married to your husband for 11 years and you love him and your children very much. Children always come first. As a child, you and your parents were migrant workers, so you are happy that you have a place to live and do not need to move around. Because of the migrant work, you didn't go past the sixth grade. Your husband works on a construction crew laying concrete. When it's not raining and when there's plenty of building, he has lots of work. Sometimes, though, he will go two or three weeks with no work and, therefore, no money. Your parents live in your town, and they try to help you when times are bad. You get food stamps to help out. You go to Mass every Sunday, and often on weekends you go to your parents' place with your children and brothers and sisters. Your husband is a good man, and he loves his children. On a good week he will bring home $400.

Current Situation

Maria comes home and says she has to do a salt map. You have just spent all the money for the week on food—and she needs five pounds of flour, two pounds of salt, and a piece of board to put it on. She also needs to get information from an encyclopedia, whatever that is. The car has broken down and will require $100 for parts. The baby is sick, and medicine will be $30. It has rained for two weeks, and your husband hasn't had any work or pay.

The teacher has asked Maria to stay after school and be in an academic contest. You expect her to get married and have children just as you have. But for now you need her to help you with the children.

What resources do Maria and Noemi have? Check yes by the resources that are present, check no by the ones that are not, or check question mark where the resources are uncertain.

RESOURCES — SCENARIO #4	YES	NO	?
Financial			
Emotional			
Mental			
Spiritual			
Physical			
Support systems			
Knowledge of middle-class hidden rules			
Role models			

SCENARIO #5: EILEEN AND WISTERIA

Background

Eileen is a 10-year-old Caucasian girl who lives with her 70-year-old grandmother, Wisteria, who is on Social Security. Eileen doesn't know who her father is. Her mother has been arrested four times for prostitution and/or drug possession in the last two years. About once a year, Mother sobers up for a month and wants Eileen back as her child.

You are Eileen's grandmother, Wisteria. You get about $150 a week from Social Security. Your daughter, Eileen's mother, has been in trouble for years. You have given up on her, and you couldn't stand to see Eileen in a foster home, so you have taken her into your home. Eileen's mother was never sure who the father was; she is a drug addict and has been arrested frequently. One of her various pimps or boyfriends usually gets her out of jail. Once a year, when she sobers up for a short period of time, she gives Eileen lots of attention and then leaves. The last time she came and left, Eileen cried and cried and said she never wanted to see her mother again. You have a little money in savings, but you don't want to use it yet. Your house is paid for, and you have a decent car. You worry what will happen to Eileen if you get sick or die, and you pray each day to live until Eileen is 18. You don't see as well as you once did. All your relatives are either dead or distant. Every Sunday you and Eileen go to the United Methodist Church where you have been a member for 40 years.

Current Situation

Eileen comes home from school with an assigned project. She must do a family history and interview as many relatives as possible. You aren't sure what to say to Eileen.

The teacher tells you at a conference that Eileen has an imaginary friend whom she talks to a great deal during the day. The teacher recommends that you seek counseling for Eileen. She knows a counselor who would charge only $40 a session. She also comments that Eileen's clothes are old-fashioned and that she doesn't fit in very well with the other students. You don't tell the teacher that you make Eileen's clothes. The teacher suggests that you let Eileen have friends over so she can socialize, but you don't know if anyone would come—or if you could stand the noise.

What are Eileen and Wisteria's resources? Check yes by the resources that are present, check no by the ones that are not, or check question mark where the resources are uncertain.

RESOURCES — SCENARIO #5	YES	NO	?
Financial			
Emotional			
Mental			
Spiritual			
Physical			
Support systems			
Knowledge of middle-class hidden rules			
Role models			

SCENARIO #6: JUAN AND RAMON

Background

Juan is a 6-year-old Hispanic boy who lives with his uncle Ramón. Juan's father was killed in a gang-related killing. His uncle is angry about the death of Juan's father. When his uncle is not around, Juan stays with his grandmother, who speaks no English. The uncle makes his living selling drugs but is very respectful toward his mother.

You are Juan's uncle, Ramón, a 25-year-old Hispanic male. You doubt that you will live many more years because you know that most of the people like you are either dead or in jail. You are angry. Your brother, Juan's father, was killed by a rival gang two years ago when Juan was 4. Juan is your godchild, and you will defend him with your blood. Juan's mother was a piece of white trash and wouldn't take care of Juan like a good mother should. She is in jail now for gang-related activities. You leave Juan with your mother often because the activities you're involved in are too dangerous to have Juan along. You are a leader in your gang and sell drugs as well. Your mother speaks only Spanish, but you have taught Juan to be very respectful toward her. She goes to Mass every Sunday and takes Juan with her when she can. You make $1,000 a week on the average.

Current Situation

Juan comes home with a notice about a parent-teacher conference. You are away, hiding from the police. Grandmother cannot read Spanish or English.

The rival gang has killed another one of your gang members. This has forced you to be away from Juan more than you would like. Plans are that you will kill the leader of the rival gang, but then you will need to go to Mexico for some time to hide. You are thinking about taking Juan with you because he is all in the world that you love. You are stockpiling money. You don't want to take him out of school, but he is only 6; he can catch up. You don't think you'll live past 30, and you want to have time with him.

What resources do Juan and Ramón have? Check yes by the resources that are present, check no by the ones that are not, or check question mark where the resources are uncertain.

RESOURCES — SCENARIO #6	YES	NO	?
Financial			
Emotional			
Mental			
Spiritual			
Physical			
Support systems			
Knowledge of middle-class hidden rules			
Role models			

SCENARIO #7: SALLY AND SUEANN

Background

Sally is an 8-year-old Caucasian girl whose mother, SueAnn, has been married and divorced twice. Her mother works two jobs and does not receive child support. An older sister is pregnant. Sally has two stepsiblings—one younger and one older. The current stepfather's favorite child is the youngest child, a son. The stepfather is laid off right now.

You are Sally's mother, SueAnn, a 33-year-old female. You are on your third marriage. You have four children by four different men. You are working two jobs right now because your current husband has been laid off. He is supposed to be taking care of the kids, but he doesn't like to be tied down. You got pregnant when you were a senior in high school, so you were unable to finish school. You knew who the father was, but he changed his mind and wouldn't marry you. You kept the child, and she is now 15 and pregnant. Your second child is Sally, and she is 8 years old. Between the two jobs, you bring home about $400 a week, and you are exhausted. You make the girls cook and clean. You are very tired. Lately you and your husband have been fighting a lot. Your mother and father are divorced and live in the same town that you do. You remember how much you loved to dance country-western and party. All you wish for now is sleep. You may have to move again soon because you're so far behind on the bills.

Current Situation

You get a call at work. You had let your husband drop you off at work because he was going to fix the muffler. Your husband is now in jail. He was caught driving while intoxicated. This is the second time he has been caught. You need $500 to pay the bondsman to get him out of jail. Furthermore, he was driving your car, which didn't have insurance. They have towed the car, and the towing bill is $80. Each day it's impounded it will cost you $40 in parking fees, and you can't get the car out until you have proof of insurance.

When and if your husband gets out of jail, he will need to see the probation officer, which will cost him $60 each visit.

Your pregnant daughter needs $400 to pay the doctor so that he will keep seeing her. You have told her she needs to go to the clinic where the service is free. However, the wait is usually three to four hours, and she misses a half day of school. There is also the problem of getting her there. It's in a bad part of town, and it will be dark before you can get there to pick her up.

The bill collector calls you at work and tells you he is going to take you to court for overdue electric bills at the last place you lived. You now live in an apartment where the utilities are paid, but you are behind on your rent by a month. You were OK until your husband got laid off. You are out of birth-control pills. To refill the prescription, you have to go to the clinic and wait three to four hours, and you can't take that much time off work. Also, you need $20 for the birth-control pills. Lately your husband has been looking at Sally in ways that you don't like. But you are so tired.

What are Sally and SueAnn's resources? Check yes by the resources that are present, check no by the ones that are not, or check question mark where the resources are uncertain.

RESOURCES — SCENARIO #7	YES	NO	?
Financial			
Emotional			
Mental			
Spiritual			
Physical			
Support systems			
Knowledge of middle-class hidden rules			
Role models			

DISCUSSION OF SCENARIOS

Significantly, each scenario illustrates a variance in the amount and kinds of resources available, as well as a variation on the theme of poverty. In marking the scenarios, this would be the manner in which the resources might be identified.

RESOURCES	#1	#2	#3	#4	#5	#6	#7
Financial	N	N	N	N	?	Y	Y
Emotional	N	N	Y	Y	?	N	N
Mental	Y	N	Y	Y	Y	Y	Y
Spiritual	N	N	Y	Y	Y	Y	N
Physical	Y	Y	Y	Y	Y	Y	Y
Support systems	N	N	Y	Y	Y	Y	N
Knowledge of middle-class hidden rules	Y	N	Y	N	Y	N	N
Role models	?	N	Y	Y	?	N	N

Knowledge of the hidden rules is marked in relationship to the knowledge base the individual has about middle-class rules. Each of the scenarios has aspects that are unique to poverty.

For example, the jail incident in the SueAnn scenario is one. For many individuals who live in poverty, jail is a part of their lives on a fairly regular basis for several reasons. First of all, if an individual is in generational poverty, organized society is viewed with distrust, even distaste. The line between what is legal and illegal is thin and often crossed. A lack of resources means that the individual will need to spend periods of time in jail for crossing those lines because he/she does not have the resources to avoid it. The reality is that middle class and upper class also cross the lines, but not with the frequency of those in poverty. In addition, the upper and middle classes usually have the resources to avoid jail. The poor simply see jail as a part of life and not necessarily always bad. Local jails provide food and shelter and, as a general rule, are not as violent or dangerous as state incarceration. SueAnn will probably get her husband out of jail because relationships are also more important in generational poverty than is money.

Another example of a poverty characteristic is the incident with Oprah at church where she receives the extra money and is immediately besieged with requests. One of the hidden rules of poverty is that any extra money is shared. Middle class puts a great deal of emphasis on being self-sufficient. In poverty, the clear understanding is that one will never get ahead, so when extra money is available, it is either shared or immediately spent. There are always emergencies and needs; one might as well enjoy the moment. Oprah will share the money; she has no choice. If she does not, the next time she is in need, she will be left in the cold. It is the hidden rule of the support system. In poverty, people are possessions, and people can rely only on each other. It is absolutely imperative that the needs of an individual come first. After all, that is all you have—people.

The discipline incident in "Otis and Vangie" is included because another aspect of generational poverty is that discipline is about penance and forgiveness, not about change. The mother is the most powerful figure in generational poverty. Not only does she control the limited resources, she is also the "keeper of the soul." She dispenses penance and forgiveness. The typical pattern in poverty for discipline is to verbally chastise the child, or physically beat the child, then forgive and feed him/her. The hidden rules about food in poverty is that food is equated with love. In the final analysis, all you have are people. How do you show people that you love them? You give them food so they can continue to live. One of the mistakes educators make is to misunderstand the role of punishment in generational poverty. As stated, punishment is not about change, it's about penance and forgiveness. Individuals in poverty usually have a strong belief in fate and destiny. Therefore, to expect changed behavior after a parent-teacher conference is, in most cases, a false hope.

The Juan/Ramón scenario is included to make some points about the role of violence and gangs in poverty. Gangs are a type of support system. They provide virtually all of the resources needed for survival. Fighting and physical violence are a part of poverty. People living in poverty need to be able to defend themselves physically, or they need someone to be their protector. Middle class uses space to deal with conflict and disagreement, i.e. they go to a different room and cool off; they purchase enough land so they are not encroached upon; they live in neighborhoods where people keep their distance. But in poverty, separation is not an option. The only way to defend turf is physically. Also, individuals in poverty are seldom going to call the police, for two reasons: First, the police may be looking for them; second, the police are going to be slow to respond. So why bother calling?

The Eileen/Wisteria scenario is included because of the growing number of children living with grandparents—and the effect this has on the emotional resources of the children. Emotional resources come from observing how role models deal with adverse situations and social interactions. Eileen will come out of the situation knowing that she doesn't want to be like her mother, but also that she doesn't want to be like her grandmother. So it will be difficult for her to identify an appropriate female role model. To have emotional resources that are healthy, one needs to have an identity. One uses role models to build that identity. Because of the limited financial resources of her grandmother, Eileen's access to appropriate role models will be limited to church and school.

The John/Adele scenario highlights the number of children who are in situational poverty because of divorce. Adele is making the slide from middle class to poverty, and she doesn't know the rules of poverty. Adele is an example of what happens when an individual allows her difficulties to erode her emotional resources. Because of her alcoholism, she is emotionally weak. (The reverse is also true, i.e., her emotional weakness leads to her dependence on alcohol.) Of all the resources, emotional resources seem to be paramount in maintaining a lifestyle with some semblance of order. When emotional resources are absent, the slide to poverty is almost guaranteed. But because her financial resources are limited, she must learn the rules of generational poverty. And one of the rules in generational poverty for women is this: you may need to use your body for survival. After all, that is all that is truly yours. Sex will bring in money and favors. Values are important, but they don't put food on the table—or bring relief from intense pressure. So Adele will probably go out with the mechanic, for two reasons: (1) She can get her car fixed and (2) she can have an evening out on the town.

Maria and Noemi are included because they represent the classic Hispanic pattern of poverty. In the Hispanic poverty pattern, the majority of families are two-parent. As can be seen, of all the scenarios Maria and Noemi have more resources than any of the others.

In conclusion, the resources that individuals have vary significantly from situation to situation. Poverty is more about other resources than it is about money. The other resources are those that educators can influence greatly.

WHAT DOES THIS INFORMATION MEAN IN THE SCHOOL OR WORK SETTING?

- ■ Resources of students and adults should be analyzed before dispensing advice or seeking solutions to the situation. What may seem to be very workable suggestions from a middle-class point of view may be virtually impossible given the resources available to those in poverty.

- ■ Educators have tremendous opportunities to influence some of the non-financial resources that make such a difference in students' lives. For example, it costs nothing to be an appropriate role model.

CHAPTER 2

The Role of Language and Story

To better understand poverty, one must understand three aspects of language: registers of language, discourse patterns, and story structure. Many of the key issues for schools and businesses are related to these three patterns that often are different in poverty than they are in middle class.

REGISTERS OF LANGUAGE

Every language in the world has five registers (Joos, 1967). These registers are the following:

REGISTER	EXPLANATION
FROZEN	Language that is always the same. For example: Lord's Prayer, wedding vows, etc.
FORMAL	The standard sentence syntax and word choice of work and school. Has complete sentences and specific word choice.
CONSULTATIVE	Formal register when used in conversation. Discourse pattern not quite as direct as formal register.
CASUAL	Language between friends and is characterized by a 400- to 800-word vocabulary. Word choice general and not specific. Conversation dependent upon non-verbal assists. Sentence syntax often incomplete.
INTIMATE	Language between lovers or twins. Language of sexual harassment.

RULE: Joos found that one can go one register down in the same conversation, and that is socially accepted. However, to drop two registers or more in the same conversation is to be socially offensive.

How then does this register impact students from poverty? First of all, the work of Dr. Maria Montano-Harmon (1991) found that the majority (of the students in her research) of minority students and poor students do not have access to formal register at home. As a matter of fact, these students cannot use formal register. The problem is that all the state tests—SAT, ACT, etc.—are in formal register. It is further complicated by the fact that to get a well-paying job, it is expected that one will be able to use formal register. Ability to use formal register is a hidden rule of the middle class. The inability to use it will knock one out of an interview in two or three minutes. The use of formal register, on the other hand, allows one to score well on tests and do well in school and higher education.

This use of formal register is further complicated by the fact that these students do not have the vocabulary or the knowledge of sentence structure and syntax to use formal register. When student conversations in the casual register are observed, much of the meaning comes not from the word choices, but from the non-verbal assists. To be asked to communicate in writing without the non-verbal assists is an overwhelming and formidable task, which most of them try to avoid. It has very little meaning for them.

DISCOURSE PATTERNS IN FORMAL AND CASUAL REGISTER

This pattern of registers is connected to the second issue: the patterns of discourse. Discourse will be discussed here with two different meanings. The first meaning is the manner in which the information is organized. In the formal register of English, the pattern is to get straight to the point. In casual register, the pattern is to go around and around and finally get to the point. For students who have no access to formal register, educators become frustrated with the tendency of these students to meander almost endlessly through a topic. It is simply the manner in which information is organized in casual register.

LANGUAGE ACQUISITION IN PRIMARY AND SECONDARY DISCOURSE

The other meaning associated with discourse is the notion of primary and secondary discourse issues (Gee, 1987). Primary discourse is the language an individual first acquired. Secondary discourse is the language of the larger society that the individual must be able to use to function in the larger society. For example, if a student has as his/her primary discourse casual register of Spanish, then he/she must also learn formal register of English in order to fully negotiate and participate in the larger American society. Gee points out that students do much better in school when their primary discourse is the same as their secondary discourse.

RAMIFICATIONS

Gee proceeds to make a distinction between acquisition and learning. Acquisition is the best and most natural way to learn a language and is simply the immersion in, and constant interaction with, that language. Learning is the direct-teaching of a language and usually is at a more metacognitive level. However, what Gee does not talk about is the following: acquisition of language only occurs when there is a significant relationship. That then leads to the next question: To what extent can a formal institution create significant relationships? Just think . . . would you learn to use sign language well if there were no significant relationship that called for that usage? Would you learn to speak Chinese well if there were no significant relationship?

Therefore, when we ask students to move from casual to formal register, we almost need to direct-teach it. Natural acquisition of formal register would require a significant relationship.

Montano-Harmon (1991) found that for students to move from casual-register English to formal-register English required them to translate because the word choice, sentence syntax, and discourse pattern are different. This translation becomes much more meaningful if there is a significant relationship. However, if there is not a significant relationship, then the instruction must be more direct.

PATTERNS OF DISCOURSE

In the oral-language tradition in which the casual register operates, the pattern of discourse is quite different. Discourse is defined as the organizational pattern of information (see graphic representations below).

Formal-Register Discourse Pattern

Speaker or writer gets straight to the point.

Casual-Register Discourse Pattern

Writer or speaker goes around the issue before finally coming to the point.

How does this make a difference for students and teachers? First of all, parent-teacher conferences tend to be misunderstood on both sides. Teachers want to get right to the point; parents, particularly those from poverty, need to beat around the bush first. When teachers cut the conversation and get right to the point, parents view that as being rude and non-caring. Second, writing becomes particularly difficult for students because they tend to circle the mulberry bush and not meet the standard organizational pattern of getting to the point. This discourse pattern is coupled with a third pattern, that of story structure (see next page).

STORY STRUCTURE

Formal-Register Story Structure

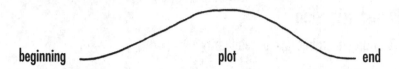

The formal-register story structure starts at the beginning of the story and goes to the end in a chronological or accepted narrative pattern. The most important part of the story is the plot.

Casual-Register Story Structure

The casual-register story structure begins with the end of the story first or the part with the greatest emotional intensity. The story is told in vignettes, with audience participation in between. The story ends with a comment about the character and his/her value. The most important part of the story is the characterization.

CINDERELLA

To understand this story structure better, the story of Cinderella will be told both ways.

Formal-Register Version
(The story is abbreviated because of familiarity.)

Once upon a time, there was a girl named Cinderella. She was very happy, and she lived with her father. Her father remarried a woman who had three daughters. When Cinderella's father died, her stepmother treated Cinderella very badly and, in fact, made her the maid for herself and her three daughters. At the same time in this land, the King decided that it was time for the Prince to get married. So, he sent a summons to all the people in the kingdom to come to a ball. Cinderella was not allowed to go, but was forced to help her stepsisters and stepmother get ready for the ball. After they left for the ball, and as Cinderella was crying on the hearth, her fairy godmother came and, with her magic wand, gave Cinderella a beautiful dress, glass slippers, and a stagecoach made from pumpkins and mice. She then sent Cinderella to the ball in style. There was one stipulation: She had to be back home by midnight.

At the ball the Prince was completely taken with Cinderella and danced with her all evening. As the clock began striking midnight, Cinderella remembered what the fairy godmother had said and fled from the dance. All she left was one of her glass slippers.

The Prince held a big search, using the glass slipper as a way to identify the missing woman. He finally found Cinderella; she could wear the glass slipper. He married her, and they lived happily ever after.

Casual-Register Version
(Italicized type indicates the narrator; plain type indicates audience participation.)

Well, you know Cinderella married the Prince, in spite of that old nasty stepmother.

Pointy eyes, that one. Old hag!

Good thing she had a fairy godmother or she never would've made it to the ball.

Lucky thing! God bless her ragged tail! Wish I had me a fairy godmother.

And to think she nearly messed up big time by staying 'til the clock was striking 12. After all the fairy godmother had done for her.

Um, um. She shoulda known better. Eyes too full of the Prince, they were. They didn't call him the Prince for no reason.

When she got to the ball, her stepsisters and stepmother didn't even recognize her she was so beautiful without those rags.

Served 'em right, no-good jealous hags.

The Prince just couldn't quit dancing with her, just couldn't take his eyes off her. He had finally found his woman.

Lucky her! Lucky him! Sure wish life was a fairy tale. Kinda like the way I met Charlie. Ha ha.

The way she arrived was something else—a couch and horseman—really fancy. Too bad that when she ran out of there as the clock struck 12 all that was left was a pumpkin rolling away and four mice!

What a surprise for the mice!

Well, he has to find her because his heart is broken. So he takes the glass slipper and hunts for her—and her old wicked stepmother, of course, is hiding her.

What a prize! Aren't they all?

But he finds her and marries her. Somebody as good as Cinderella deserved that.

Sure hope she never invited that stepmother to her castle. Should make her the maid!!

■ ■ ■ ■ ■ ■

As is readily apparent, the second story structure is far more entertaining, more participatory and exhibits a richness of character, humor, and feeling absent from the first version. The first version has sequence, order, cause and effect, and a conclusion: all skills necessary for problem-solving, inference, etc.

Cognitive studies indicate that story structure is a way that the brain stores memories. Given the first story structure, memories would be stored more sequentially, and thinking patterns would follow story structure. Feuerstein (1980) describes the episodic, nearly random memory and its adverse effects on thinking.

WHAT CAN SCHOOLS DO TO ADDRESS CASUAL REGISTER, DISCOURSE PATTERNS, AND STORY STRUCTURE?

Because there is such a direct link between achievement and language, it must be addressed. The following suggestions are not exhaustive, but rather a place to begin.

1. Have students write in casual register, then translate into formal register. (To get examples of casual register down on paper, ask them to write the way they talk.)

2. Establish as part of a discipline plan a requirement that students learn how to express their displeasure in formal register and therefore not be reprimanded.

3. Use graphic organizers to show patterns of discourse.

4. In the classroom, tell stories both ways. Tell the story using the formal-register story structure, then tell the story with the casual-register structure. Talk about the stories: how they stay the same, and how they're different.

5. Encourage participation in the writing and telling of stories.

6. Use stories in math, social studies, and science to develop concepts.

7. Make up stories with the students that can be used to guide behavior.

WHAT DOES THIS INFORMATION MEAN IN THE SCHOOL OR WORK SETTING?

- Formal register needs to be directly taught.

- Casual register needs to be recognized as the primary discourse for many students.

- Discourse patterns need to be directly taught.

- Both story structures need to be used as a part of classroom instruction.

- Discipline that occurs when a student uses the inappropriate register should be a time for instruction in the appropriate register.

- Students need to be told how much the formal register affects their ability to get a well-paying job.

CHAPTER 3

Hidden Rules Among Classes

Hidden rules are the unspoken cues and habits of a group. Distinct cueing systems exist between and among groups and economic classes. Generally, in America, that notion is recognized for racial and ethnic groups, but not particularly for economic groups. There are many hidden rules to examine. The ones examined here are those that have the most impact on achievement in schools and success in the workplace.

But first . . .

A LITTLE QUIZ

Take the quiz on the next three pages, putting a check mark by all the things you know how to do.

Could You Survive in Poverty?

Put a check by each item you know how to do.

❑ 1. I know which churches and sections of town have the best rummage sales.

❑ 2. I know which rummage sales have "bag sales" and when.

❑ 3. I know which grocery stores' garbage bins can be accessed for thrown-away food.

❑ 4. I know how to get someone out of jail.

❑ 5. I know how to physically fight and defend myself physically.

❑ 6. I know how to get a gun, even if I have a police record.

❑ 7. I know how to keep my clothes from being stolen at the Laundromat.

❑ 8. I know what problems to look for in a used car.

❑ 9. I know how to live without a checking account.

❑ 10. I know how to live without electricity and a phone.

❑ 11. I know how to use a knife as scissors.

❑ 12. I can entertain a group of friends with my personality and my stories.

❑ 13. I know what to do when I don't have money to pay the bills.

❑ 14. I know how to move in half a day.

❑ 15. I know how to get and use food stamps or an electronic card for benefits.

❑ 16. I know where the free medical clinics are.

❑ 17. I am very good at trading and bartering.

❑ 18. I can get by without a car.

Could You Survive in Middle Class?

Put a check by each item you know how to do.

☐ 1. I know how to get my children into Little League, piano lessons, soccer, etc.

☐ 2. I know how to properly set a table.

☐ 3. I know which stores are most likely to carry the clothing brands my family wears.

☐ 4. My children know the best name brands in clothing.

☐ 5. I know how to order in a nice restaurant.

☐ 6. I know how to use a credit card, checking account, and savings account—and I understand an annuity. I understand term life insurance, disability insurance, and 20/80 medical insurance policy, as well as house insurance, flood insurance, and replacement insurance.

☐ 7. I talk to my children about going to college.

☐ 8. I know how to get one of the best interest rates on my new-car loan.

☐ 9. I understand the difference among the principal, interest, and escrow statements on my house payment.

☐ 10. I know how to help my children with their homework and do not hesitate to call the school if I need additional information.

☐ 11. I know how to decorate the house for the different holidays.

☐ 12. I know how to get a library card.

☐ 13. I know how to use most of the tools in the garage.

☐ 14. I repair items in my house almost immediately when they break— or know a repair service and call it.

Could You Survive in Wealth?

Put a check by each item you know how to do.

❑ 1. I can read a menu in French, English, and another language.

❑ 2. I have several favorite restaurants in different countries of the world.

❑ 3. During the holidays, I know how to hire a decorator to identify the appropriate themes and items with which to decorate the house.

❑ 4. I know who my preferred financial advisor, legal service, designer, domestic-employment service, and hairdresser are.

❑ 5. I have at least two residences that are staffed and maintained.

❑ 6. I know how to ensure confidentiality and loyalty from my domestic staff.

❑ 7. I have at least two or three "screens" that keep people whom I do not wish to see away from me.

❑ 8. I fly in my own plane or the company plane.

❑ 9. I know how to enroll my children in the preferred private schools.

❑ 10. I know how to host the parties that "key" people attend.

❑ 11. I am on the boards of at least two charities.

❑ 12. I know the hidden rules of the Junior League.

❑ 13. I support or buy the work of a particular artist.

❑ 14. I know how to read a corporate financial statement and analyze my own financial statements.

The first point about this exercise is that if you fall mostly in the middle class, the assumption is that everyone knows these things. However, if you did not know many of the items for the other classes, the exercise points out how many of the hidden rules are taken for granted by a particular class, which assumes they are a given for everyone. What, then, are the hidden rules? The chart on pages 42 and 43 gives an overview of some of the major hidden rules among the classes of poverty, middle class, and wealth.

Several explanations and stories may help explain parts of the quiz and this chart. The bottom line or driving force against which decisions are made is important to note. For example, in one school district, the faculty had gone together to buy a refrigerator for a family who did not have one. About three weeks later, the children in the family were gone for a week. When the students returned, the teachers asked where they had been. The answer was that the family had gone camping because they were so stressed. What had they used for money to go camping? Proceeds from the sale of the refrigerator, of course. The bottom line in generational poverty is entertainment and relationships. In middle class, the criteria against which most decisions are made relate to work and achievement. In wealth, it is the ramifications of the financial, social, and political connections that have the weight.

Being able physically to fight or have someone who is willing to fight for you is important to survival in poverty. Yet, in middle class, being able to use words as tools to negotiate conflict is crucial. Many times the fists are used in poverty because the words are neither available nor respected.

The one deep experience that distinguishes the social rich
from the merely rich and those below is their schooling,
and with it, all the associations, the sense and sensibility, to
which this education routine leads throughout their lives.
As a selection and training place of the upper classes,
both old and new, the private school is a unifying influence,
a force for the nationalization of the upper classes.

– C. Wright Mills, *The Power Elite*

Hidden Rules Among Classes

	POVERTY
POSSESSIONS	People.
MONEY	To be used, spent.
PERSONALITY	Is for entertainment. Sense of humor is highly valued.
SOCIAL EMPHASIS	Social inclusion of people he/she likes.
FOOD	Key question: Did you have enough? Quantity important.
CLOTHING	Clothing valued for individual style and expression of personality.
TIME	Present most important. Decisions made for moment based on feelings or survival.
EDUCATION	Valued and revered as abstract but not as reality.
DESTINY	Believes in fate. Cannot do much to mitigate chance.
LANGUAGE	Casual register. Language is about survival.
FAMILY STRUCTURE	Tends to be matriarchal.
WORLD VIEW	Sees world in terms of local setting.
LOVE	Love and acceptance conditional, based upon whether individual is liked.
DRIVING FORCES	Survival, relationships, entertainment.
HUMOR	About people and sex.

MIDDLE CLASS	WEALTH
Things.	One-of-a-kind objects, legacies, pedigrees.
To be managed.	To be conserved, invested.
Is for acquisition and stability. Achievement is highly valued.	Is for connections. Financial, political, social connections are highly valued.
Emphasis is on self-governance and self-sufficiency.	Emphasis is on social exclusion.
Key question: Did you like it? Quality important.	Key question: Was it presented well? Presentation important.
Clothing valued for its quality and acceptance into norm of middle class. Label important.	Clothing valued for its artistic sense and expression. Designer important.
Future most important. Decisions made against future ramifications.	Traditions and history most important. Decisions made partially on basis of tradition and decorum.
Crucial for climbing success ladder and making money.	Necessary tradition for making and maintaining connections.
Believes in choice. Can change future with good choices now.	Noblesse oblige.
Formal register. Language is about negotiation.	Formal register. Language is about networking.
Tends to be patriarchal.	Depends on who has money.
Sees world in terms of national setting.	Sees world in terms of international view.
Love and acceptance conditional and based largely upon achievement.	Love and acceptance conditional and related to social standing and connections.
Work, achievement.	Financial, political, social connections.
About situations.	About social faux pas.

One of the biggest difficulties in getting out of poverty is managing money and just the general information base around money. How can you manage something you've never had? Money is seen in poverty as an expression of personality and is used for entertainment and relationships. The notion of using money for security is truly grounded in the middle and wealthy classes.

The question in the quiz about using a knife as scissors was put there to illustrate the lack of tools available to those in poverty. Tools in many ways are one of the identifiers of middle class—from the kitchen to the garage. Therefore, the notion of maintaining property and repairing items is dependent upon having tools. When they are not available, things are not repaired or maintained. Students do not have access to scissors, pens, paper, pencils, rulers, etc., which may be part of an assignment.

One of the biggest differences among the classes is how "the world" is defined for them. Wealthy individuals view the international scene as their world. As one told me, "My favorite restaurant is in Brazil." Middle class tends to see the world in terms of a national picture, while poverty sees the world in its immediate locale. Several fourth-grade poor students told us when they were writing to the prompt, *How is life in Houston different from life in Baytown*? (Baytown is 20 minutes from Houston), "They don't have TVs in Houston."

In wealth, to be introduced or accepted, one must have an individual already approved by that group make the introductions. Yet to stand back and not introduce yourself in a middle-class setting is not the accepted norm. And in poverty it is not unusual to have a comment made about the individual before he/she is ever introduced.

The discussion could continue about hidden rules. The key point is that hidden rules govern so much of our immediate assessment of an individual and his/her capabilities. These are often the factors that keep an individual from moving upward in a career—or even getting the position in the first place.

WHAT DOES THIS INFORMATION MEAN IN THE SCHOOL OR WORK SETTING?

- Assumptions made about individuals' intelligence and approaches to the school and/or work setting may relate more to their understanding of hidden rules.

- Students need to be taught the hidden rules of middle class— not in denigration of their own but rather as another set of rules that can be used if they so choose.

- Many of the attitudes that students and parents bring with them are an integral part of their culture and belief systems. Middle-class solutions should not necessarily be imposed when other, more workable, solutions might be found.

- An understanding of the culture and values of poverty will lessen the anger and frustration that educators may periodically feel when dealing with these students and parents.

- Most of the students that I have talked to in poverty do not believe they are poor, even when they are on welfare. Most of the wealthy adults I have talked to do not believe they are wealthy; they will usually cite someone who has more than they do.

CHAPTER 4

Characteristics of Generational Poverty

Life is lived in common, but not in community.

– Michael Harrington,
Four Horsemen

Generational poverty is defined as having been in poverty for at least two generations; however, the patterns begin to surface much sooner than two generations if the family lives with others who are from generational poverty. *Situational poverty* is defined as a lack of resources due to a particular event (i.e., a death, chronic illness, divorce, etc.). Generational poverty has its own culture, hidden rules, and belief systems. One of the key indicators of whether it is generational or situational poverty is the prevailing attitude. Often the attitude in generational poverty is that society owes one a living. In situational poverty the attitude is often one of pride and a refusal to accept charity. Individuals in situational poverty often bring more resources with them to the situation than those in generational poverty. Of particular importance is the use of formal register.

What, then, makes generational poverty so different from the middle class? How is it that school is such an unsatisfactory experience for many students from poverty? Several of these differences were mentioned in the last chapter on hidden rules. To examine the differences, a case study will be used.

CASE STUDY: WALTER (Caucasian male)

Italicized type indicates the narrator; plain type indicates comments from various listeners. Names have been changed to protect the girl.

AS THE STORY WOULD BE TOLD IN POVERTY . . .
PROBABLY BY A RELATIVE OR NEIGHBOR:

Well, you know Walter got put away for 37 years. Him being 48 and all. He'll probably die in jail. Just couldn't leave his hands off that 12-year-old Susie.

Dirty old man. Bodding's gonna whup his tail.

Already did. You know Bodding was waiting for him in jail and beat the living daylights out of him.

In jail?

Yeah, Bodding got caught for possession. Had $12,000 on him when they arrested him.

Golly, wish I had been there to cash in!!!! (laughter) A man's gotta make a living!

Susie being blind and all—I can see why Bodding beat the daylights out of Walter. Lucky he didn't get killed, old Walter is.

Too bad her momma is no good.

She started the whole thing! Susie's momma goes over there and argues with Bodding.

Ain't they divorced?

Yeah, and she's got Walter working for her, repairing her house or something.

Or something, I bet. What's she got in her house that's worth fixing?

Anyway, she goes over to Bodding's house to take the lawnmower . . .

I reckon so as Walter can mow the yard?? I bet that's the first time old Walter has ever broken a sweat! Reminds me of the time I saw Walter thinking about taking a job. All that thinking and he had to get drunk. He went to jail that time, too—a felony, I think it was. So many of those DWIs. Judge told him he was egregious. Walter said he wasn't greasy—he took a bath last week!!! (laughter)

Bodding and Susie's momma got in a fight, so she tells Walter to take Susie with him.

Lordy, her elevator must not go all the way to the top!! Didn't she know about him getting arrested for enticing a minor???

With Susie blind and all. And she sends Susie with Walter?

She sure don't care about her babies.

Well, Walter's momma was there 'cause Walter lives with his momma, seeing as how he can't keep no job.

Ain't his other brother there?

Yeah, and him 41 years old. That poor momma sure has her burdens to bear. And then her 30-year-old daughter, Susie's momma, at home, too. You know Susie's momma lost custody of her kids. Walter gets these videos, you know. Those adult videos. Heavy breathing! (laughter)

Some of them are more fun to listen to than look at! (laughter) Those people in the videos are des-per-ate!!

Anyway, he puts those on and then carries Susie to his room and tells her she wants him—and describes all his sex-u-al exploits!!

Golly, he must be a loooooooooover. (laughter) He should be shot. I'd kill him if he did that to my kid!!

Then he lets his fingers do the walking.

Kinda like the Yellow Pages! (laughter)

I guess he didn't do anything with his "thang," according to Miss Rosie who went to that trial every day. And Susie begging him to stop so many times.

Probably couldn't do anything with it; that's why he needs to listen to that heavy breathing! Pant! Pant! (laughter) What a no-count, low-down creep. I'll pay Bodding to kill him!!

Bodding says the only way Walter is coming out of jail is in a pine box.

Don't blame him myself.

Yeah, Miss Rosie said Walter's momma said at the trial that the door to Walter's room was open and there ain't no way Walter could have done that. That she is a good Christian momma and she don't put up with that.

Oh Lordy, did God strike her dead on the spot, or is she still alive??? I'd be afraid of ending up in eternal damnation for telling a story like that!

Miss Rosie said her 12-year-old nephew testified that the door was closed and his grandma told him to say it was open!!!!

Ooo! Ooo! Oooo! That poor baby tells the truth? His grandma's gonna make him mis-er-a-ble!!!

And then Walter's momma tells that jury that she never allows those adult videos in her house, leastways not that she pays for them!! (lots of laughter)

I bet the judge bit on that one!! How is Walter gonna get videos except for her money? Mowing yards? (more laughter) No, I bet he saves his pennies!! (laughter)

All these years she has covered for Walter. Guess she just couldn't cover no more.

Remember that time Walter got drunk and wrecked her car, and she said she was driving? And she was at the hospital at the time with a broken leg. And the judge asked her how she could be driving and in the hospital "simultaneously." And she said that's just how it was—simultaneously—she had never felt so excited in her life. (laughter) Who turned Walter in?

Well, it wasn't Susie's momma. She was busy with Skeeter, her new boyfriend. I hear he's something.

Remember that one boyfriend she had? Thought he was so smart?

Speaking of smart, that Susie sure is. Her blind and all, and she won the district spelling bee for the seventh grade this year. I hear she's in National Honor Society, whatever that is.

Wonder if it's kinda like the country club. Instead of playing golf, you just spell!!! (laughter)

Susie calls this friend of hers who tells her mother and they come and get her and take her to the police and hospital.

Some rich lady, not minding her own business, that's for sure.

Well, it was a good thing for Susie, 'cause that momma of hers sure ain't good for Susie. She don't deserve a kid like Susie. SHE oughta be the one who's blind.

Ain't that the truth. Way I see it, she already is. Just look at Skeeter!! (gales of laughter)

(The preceding was an actual court case heard in Houston, Texas, during March 1995. Italicized print indicates what came out in the trial; plain print indicates the kinds of comments that might be made by others in generational poverty.)

Using this case, check which of the following characteristics of generational poverty are present.

❑ *Background "noise":* Almost always the TV is on, no matter what the circumstance. Conversation is participatory, often with more than one person talking at a time.

❑ *Importance of personality:* Individual personality is what one brings to the setting—because money is not brought. The ability to entertain, tell stories, and have a sense of humor is highly valued.

❑ *Significance of entertainment:* When one can merely survive, then the respite from the survival is important. In fact, entertainment brings respite.

❑ *Importance of relationships:* One only has people upon whom to rely, and those relationships are important to survival. One often has favorites.

❑ *Matriarchal structure:* The mother has the most powerful position in the society if she functions as a caretaker.

❑ *Oral-language tradition:* Casual register is used for everything.

❑ *Survival orientation:* Discussion of academic topics is generally not prized. There is little room for the abstract. Discussions center around people and relationships. A job is about making enough money to survive. A job is not about a career (e.g., "I was looking for a job when I found this one").

❑ *Identity tied to lover/fighter role for men:* The key issue for males is to be a "man." The rules are rigid and a man is expected to work hard physically—and be a lover and a fighter.

❑ *Identity tied to rescuer/martyr role for women:* A "good" woman is expected to take care of and rescue her man and her children as needed.

❑ *Importance of non-verbal/kinesthetic communication:* Touch is used to communicate, as are space and non-verbal emotional information.

❑ *Ownership of people:* People are possessions. There is a great deal of fear and comment about leaving the culture and "getting above your raisings."

❑ *Negative orientation:* Failure at anything is the source of stories and numerous belittling comments.

❑ *Discipline:* Punishment is about penance and forgiveness, not change.

❑ *Belief in fate:* Destiny and fate are the major tenets of the belief system. Choice is seldom considered.

❑ *Polarized thinking:* Options are hardly ever examined. Everything is polarized; it is one way or the other. These kinds of statements are common: "I quit" and "I can't do it."

❑ *Mating dance:* The mating dance is about using the body in a sexual way and verbally and subverbally complimenting body parts. If you have few financial resources, the way you sexually attract someone is with your body.

❑ *Time:* Time occurs only in the present. The future does not exist except as a word. Time is flexible and not measured. Time is often assigned on the basis of the emotional significance and not the actual measured time.

❑ *Sense of humor:* A sense of humor is highly valued, as entertainment is one of the key aspects of poverty. Humor is almost always about people—either situations that people encounter or things people do to other people.

❑ *Lack of order/organization:* Many of the homes/apartments of people in poverty are unkempt and cluttered. Devices for organization (files, planners, etc.) don't exist.

❑ *Lives in the moment—does not consider future ramifications:* Being proactive, setting goals, and planning ahead are not a part of generational poverty. Most of what occurs is reactive and in the moment. Future implications of present actions are seldom considered.

> *Even in telling me some of those stories that involve a great deal of humiliation at the hands of hospital or welfare personnel, she usually manages to find something that's funny in the madness of it all and keeps on saying things that make both of us laugh* (in describing Mrs. Washington).
>
> – Jonathan Kozol, *Amazing Grace*

DEBRIEFING THE WALTER CASE STUDY

The Walter case study is an example of many of the issues in generational poverty. The family members all live together. Momma is still the most powerful position and these children are nearly 50. Momma will always make excuses for her children. After all, they are *her* children. The matriarchal structure and possession of people are there. She decides their guilt and punishment, not some outside authority. She leans on the self-righteous defense of being moral and Christian, but not in the middle-class sense of Christianity. For her it is simply one of unconditional love. Reality is the

present—what can be persuaded and convinced in the present. Future ramifications are not considered by anyone. Entertainment is key, whether it is
moral or not.

The neighbors' view of the situation gives more insight into the reality of
generational poverty. While there is a deep distaste for sexual abuse of children,
the story is really to make fun of Walter and his family, as well as spread the
news. Humor is used to cast aspersions on the character of Walter and his
family. In many of these stories, aspersions would also be cast on the legal
system and "rich lawyers." But there is an attitude of fate or fatalism; what are
you going to do about it? That's the way it is.

FAMILY PATTERNS IN GENERATIONAL POVERTY

One of the most confusing things about understanding generational poverty
is the family patterns. In the middle-class family, even with divorce, lineage is
fairly easy to trace because of the legal documents. In generational poverty,
on the other hand, many marital arrangements are common-law. Marriage
and divorce in a legal court are only important if there is property to distribute
or custody of children. When you were never legally married to begin with
and you have no property, why pay a lawyer for something you don't have,
don't need, and don't have the money to purchase?

In the middle class, family diagrams tend to be drawn as shown at the top
of page 55. The notion is that lineage is traceable and that a linear pattern can
be found.

In generational poverty, the mother is the center of the organization, and
the family radiates from that center. Although it can happen that the mother
is uncertain of the biological father, most of the time the father of the child is
known. The second diagram on page 55 is based on a real situation. (Names
have been changed.)

In this pattern, Jolyn has been legally married three times. Jolyn and
Husband #1 had no children. Jolyn and Husband #2 had one child, Willy.
They divorced. Husband #2 eventually married the woman he lived with
for several years, and they had a child together. She also had a son from a

DIAGRAM OF MIDDLE-CLASS FAMILY

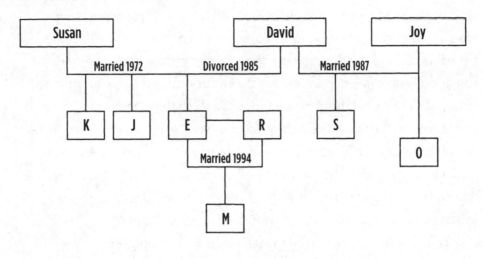

**DIAGRAM OF FAMILY FROM
GENERATIONAL POVERTY**

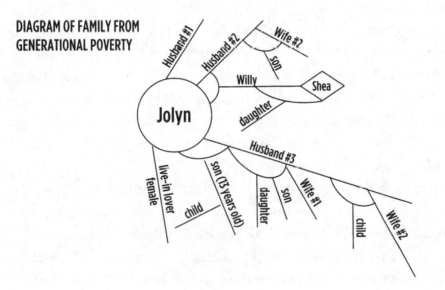

previous marriage. Willy has a common-law wife, Shea; Shea and Willy have a daughter. Jolyn and Husband #3 lived together several years before they were married, and they have a son named M.J. When M.J. was 13 he had a child with a 13-year-old girl, but that child lives with the girl's mother. Husband #3 and Jolyn divorced; Jolyn is now living with a woman in a lesbian relationship. Husband #3 is living with a younger woman who is pregnant with his child.

The mother is always at the center, though she may have multiple sexual relationships. Many of her children also will have multiple relationships, which may or may not produce children. The basic pattern is the mother at the heart of things, with nearly everyone having multiple relationships, some legal and some not. Eventually the relationships become intertwined. It wouldn't be out of the question for your sister's third husband to become your brother's ex-wife's live-in boyfriend. Also in this pattern are babies born out of wedlock to children in their early teens; these youngsters are often raised by the grandmother as her own children. For example, the oldest daughter has a child at 14. This infant becomes the youngest child in the existing family. The oldest daughter, who is actually the mother of the child, is referred to as her sister—and the relationship is a sibling one, not a mother-daughter one.

But the mother or maternal grandmother tends to keep her biological children. Because of the violence in poverty, death tends to be a prominent part of the family history. But it is also part of the family present because the deceased plays such a role in the memories of the family. It is important to note when dealing with the family patterns who is alive and who is dead— because in the discussions they are often still living (unless you, the listener, know differently).

Frequently, in the stories that are brought to school officials, the individual will tell the story in the episodic, random manner of the casual-register story structure. Key individuals are usually not referred to during the story because making reference to them isn't part of the story structure. *The most important keys to understanding the story are often the omissions.* For example, when someone says, "He left," you can pretty much predict who "he" will go stay with when there is trouble. If he is having trouble with his mother, he will go stay with an ex-wife or a girlfriend. If he is having trouble with his current wife, he will go stay with his mother. Women tend to go stay with their sisters and sometimes their mothers. Whether or not a mother or ex-wife is mentioned in the story, if the family is in generational poverty, you can be fairly certain that these are key players. You can also be fairly sure that the males are in and out—sometimes present, sometimes not, but not in any predictable pattern. Furthermore, you can know that as the male temporarily or permanently changes residences, the allegiances will change also.

Additionally within these families there tend to be multiple internal feuds. Allegiances may change overnight; favoritism is a way of life. *Who children go to stay with after school, who stays with whom when there is trouble, and who is available to deal with school issues are dependent on the current alliances and relationships at that moment.* For example, Ned comes home drunk and beats up his wife, Susan. She calls the police and escapes with the three kids to her mother's house. He goes to his mother's because she arranges to get him out of jail. His mother is not speaking to Susan because she called the cops on him and put him in jail. But Ned's mother usually keeps his kids after school until Susan gets home. Now it is Monday and Susan doesn't have any place to send the kids. So she tells them to go to her mother's house after school, which means they must go on a different bus because she doesn't know if Ned will show up at the house and be waiting for her. On Tuesday the kids again go to Susan's mom's house. But on Wednesday Ned's mom calls Susan and tells her that that no-good Ned got drunk last night and she kicked him out of her house. So now Susan and Ned's mother are good friends, and Ned is on the hot seat. So Ned goes to the apartment of his ex-wife, Jackie, because last week she decided she'd had enough of Jerry, and she was very glad to see Ned . . . And so the story continues.

The key roles in these families are fighter/lover, caretaker/rescuer, worker, storyteller, and "keeper of the soul" (i.e., dispenser of penance and forgiveness). The family patterns in generational poverty are different from the middle class. *In poverty the roles, the multiple relationships, the nature of the male identity, the ever-changing allegiances, the favoritism, and the matriarchal structure result in a different pattern.*

The economic traits which are most characteristic of the culture of poverty include the constant struggle for survival, unemployment and underemployment, low wages, a miscellany of unskilled occupations, child labor, the absence of savings, a chronic shortage of cash, the absence of food reserves in the home, the pattern of frequent buying of small quantities of food many times a day as the need arises, the pawning of personal goods, borrowing from local money lenders at usurious rates of interest, spontaneous informal credit devices (tandas) organized by neighbors, and the use of second-hand clothing and furniture.

– Oscar Lewis, *Four Horsemen*

HOW THESE CHARACTERISTICS SURFACE WITH ADULTS AND STUDENTS FROM POVERTY

Place a check mark in front of the items that describe students or adults with whom you regularly interact. They . . .

❑ get mad and quit their job/work. If they don't like the boss/ teacher, they will quit. The emphasis is on the current feeling, not the long-term ramifications.

❑ will work hard if they like you.

❑ do not use conflict-resolution skills, preferring to settle issues in verbal or physical assaults.

❑ use survival language, tending to operate out of casual register.

❑ are not emotionally reserved when angry, usually saying exactly what is on their mind.

❑ have an extreme freedom of speech, enjoy a sense of humor, use the personality to entertain, have a love of stories about people.

❑ are very independent. They won't take kindly to the "parent" voice. If their full cooperation is sought, the boss/employer needs to use the "adult" voice.

❑ periodically need time off or late arrival due to family emergencies.

❑ need emotional warmth from colleagues/boss/teacher(s) in order to feel comfortable.

❑ require a level of integrity from management, actively distrusting organizations and the people who represent the organizations. They see organizations as basically dishonest.

❑ exhibit a possessiveness about the people they really like.

❑ need a greater amount of "space" to allow for the uniqueness of their personalities.

❑ show favoritism for certain people and give them preferential treatment.

Also . . .

■ Men socialize with men and women with women. Men tend to have two social outlets: bars and work. Women with children tend to stay at home and have only other female relatives as friends, unless they work outside the home. Men tend to be loners in any other social setting and avoid those social settings. When a man and a woman are together, it is usually about a private relationship.

■ A real man is ruggedly good-looking, is a lover, can physically fight, works hard, takes no crap.

■ A real woman takes care of her man by feeding him and downplaying his shortcomings.

NOTE: In generational poverty, the primary role of a real man is to physically work hard, to be a fighter, and to be a lover. In middle class, a real man is a provider. If one follows the implications of a male identity as one who is a fighter and a lover, then one can understand why the male who takes this identity (of fighter and lover as his own) cannot have a stable life. Of the three responses to life—to flee, flow, or fight—he can only fight or flee. So when the stress gets high, he fights, then flees from the law and the people closest to him, leaving his home. Either way he is gone. When the heat dies down, he returns—to an initial welcome, then more fights. The cycle begins again.

HOW THESE CHARACTERISTICS SURFACE AT SCHOOL

Place a check mark in front of the items that describe students with whom you regularly interact. They . . .

- ❑ are very disorganized, frequently lose papers, don't have signatures, etc.

- ❑ bring many reasons why something is missing, or the paper is gone, etc.

- ❑ don't do homework.

- ❑ are physically aggressive.

- ❑ like to entertain.

- ❑ only see part of what is on the page.

- ❑ only do part of the assignment.

- ❑ can't seem to get started (no procedural self-talk).

- ❑ cannot monitor their own behavior.

- ❑ laugh when they are disciplined.

- ❑ decide whether or not they will work in your class, based on whether or not they like you.

- ❑ tell stories in the casual-register structure.

- ❑ don't know or use middle-class courtesies.

- ❑ dislike authority.

- ❑ talk back and are extremely participatory.

GENERATIONAL POVERTY

One of the reasons it is getting more and more difficult to conduct school as we have in the past is that the students who bring the middle-class culture with them are decreasing in numbers, and the students who bring the poverty culture with them are increasing in numbers. As in any demographic switch, the prevailing rules and policies eventually give way to the group with the largest numbers.

In order to better serve these students, the next several chapters have ideas about ways in which we can work with students and adults. But to do so, we must fundamentally rethink the notions we have traditionally assigned to relationships and achievement.

WHAT DOES THIS INFORMATION MEAN IN THE SCHOOL OR WORK SETTING?

- ▪ An *education* is the key to getting out of, and staying out of, generational poverty. Individuals leave poverty for one of four reasons: a goal or vision of something they want to be or have; a situation that is so painful that anything would be better; someone who "sponsors" them (i.e., an educator or spouse or mentor or role model who shows them a different way or convinces them that they could live differently); or a specific talent or ability that provides an opportunity for them.

- Being in poverty is rarely about a lack of intelligence or ability.

- Many individuals stay in poverty because they don't know there is a choice—and if they do know that, have no one to teach them hidden rules or provide resources.

- Schools are virtually the only places where students can learn the choices and rules of the middle class.

The culture of poverty has some universal characteristics which transcend regional, rural-urban, and even national differences ... There are remarkable similarities in family structure, interpersonal relations, time orientations, value systems, spending patterns, and the sense of community in lower-class settlements in London, Glasgow, Paris, Harlem, and Mexico City.

– Oscar Lewis, *Four Horsemen*

CHAPTER 5

Role Models and Emotional Resources

To understand the importance of role models and their part in the development of emotional resources, one must first briefly look at the notion of functional and dysfunctional systems. The following definitions will be used:

> A SYSTEM is a group in which individuals have rules, roles, and relationships.
>
> DYSFUNCTIONAL is the extent to which an individual cannot get his/her needs met within a system.

All systems are, to some extent, dysfunctional. A system is not equally functional or dysfunctional for each individual within a given system. The extent to which an individual must give up meeting his/her needs in order to meet the needs of another person is the extent to which the situation is dysfunctional.

Michael Dumont (1994) gives a case study of a girl named Ellie.

ELLIE

Ellie's mother, Victoria, is bedridden with multiple sclerosis and her father, Larry, is a small storekeeper. Victoria, in her rage at the disease and her distrust of Larry, attempts suicide when Ellie is 9 years old. It is Ellie's job each day when she comes home from school to count her mother's pills to make certain they are all there—and to check to see if her mother is alive.

Ellie tells Mr. Dumont that the worst part of her day is when she comes home from school and must check on her mother's well-being. When he tells Ellie that she is smart and asks her what she wants to be, she tells him she would like to be a secretary. At 13 Ellie becomes pregnant and drops out of school.

The situation is *dysfunctional* for Ellie because she must sublimate her needs to address the needs of her mother. In order for Ellie to have an appropriate developmental process emotionally, she needs to be a child, then an adolescent, then an adult. By being forced to take on an adult role earlier, she must in essence put her emotional development on hold while she functions in an adult role. Therefore, for the rest of her life, Ellie will seek to have her emotional needs met that were not met during her childhood. She almost certainly will not have the emotional resources and stamina necessary to function as an interdependent adult.

DEPENDENCE
INDEPENDENCE
INTERDEPENDENCE

To become a fully functioning adult, one moves developmentally from being dependent to being independent to being interdependent. Stephen Covey (1989) calls it *the maturity continuum*, and John Bradshaw (1988) refers to it as *becoming whole*. Regardless of the terminology, it basically means moving from being dependent on others to being able to work together with other adults, each independent of the other, but jointly, as equal partners.

Simply put, an individual operating in a dysfunctional setting is often forced to take an adult role early, and then as an adult, is literally caught between being dependent and independent. So one will see this fierce independence coupled with a crippling dependence that weakens the person to the point that he/she has few emotional resources. This roller-coaster ride up and down between dependence and independence takes a heavy toll. Bradshaw and others refer to this constant fluctuation between dependence and independence as *co-dependency*.

As Ellie's case study illustrates, the emotional resources come in part from the role models who are present for the child. When the appropriate role models are present, the child can go through the developmental stages at appropriate times and build emotional resources. Emotional resources are built in this fashion: The child watches the adult for emotional responses to a given situation and notes the continuum of behaviors that go with those responses. In Ellie's situation, her mother's response to her husband's infidelity was to create an even greater level of dependence—and to use the emotional ploy of guilt to manipulate Ellie. So what does Ellie do when she gets old enough? She creates a level of dependence on others as well (i.e., through pregnancy and going on welfare).

A child may decide that the role-model responses are not appropriate. Often what occurs then is that the child selects the opposite extreme from which to operate. What is problematic for the child is simply what is "normal"; an appropriate adult response is rarely observable. The child, therefore, is forced to guess at what "normal" or appropriate is.

> Question: Why would emotional resouces have such importance in
> school and at work?
>
> Answer: Emotional responses dictate behavior and, eventually,
> determine achievement.

Furthermore, in order to move from poverty to middle class or from middle class to wealth, one must trade off some relationships for achievement at least for a period of time. To do this, one needs emotional resources and stamina.

An *emotional memory bank* is defined as the emotions that are accessed habitually and "feel right." When a relationship is traded off for achievement, the emotional memory bank must be held in abeyance until the new "feel right" feeling can be obtained. That process sometimes take years. The driving force behind an individual holding the emotional memory bank in abeyance is usually one of four things: (1) The current situation is too painful for the individual to stay, (2) a compelling goal or vision of the future drives the individual, (3) a talent or skill takes the individual into new surroundings, or (4) a spouse or mentor provides an emotional comfort level while the individual learns the new skills/knowledge.

Emotional resources and stamina allow the individual to live with feelings other than those in the emotional memory bank. This allowance provides the individual the opportunity to seek options and examine other possibilities. As the case study shows, Ellie stays with her emotional memory bank and creates situations that "feel right."

HOW DO YOU PROVIDE EMOTIONAL RESOURCES WHEN THE STUDENT HAS NOT HAD ACCESS TO APPROPRIATE ROLE MODELS?

1. Through support systems.

2. By using appropriate discipline strategies and approaches.

3. By establishing long-term relationships (apprenticeships, mentorships) with adults who are appropriate.

4. By teaching the hidden rules.

5. By identifying options.

6. By increasing individuals' achievement level through appropriate instruction.

7. By teaching goal-setting.

WHAT DOES THIS INFORMATION MEAN IN THE SCHOOL OR WORK SETTING?

- Schools need to establish schedules and instructional arrangements that allow students to stay with the same teachers for two or more years—if mutually agreed upon.

■ Teachers and administrators are much more important as role models than has previously been addressed.

■ The development of emotional resources is crucial to student success. The greatest free resource available to schools is the role-modeling provided by teachers, administrators, and staff.

CHAPTER 6

Support Systems

Support systems are the friends, family, and backup resources that can be accessed in times of need. These systems of support tend to fall into seven general categories.

1. Coping Strategies

Coping strategies are the ways in which one copes with daily living: the disappointments, the tragedies, the triumphs. Coping strategies are ways to think about things, attitudes, self-talk, strategies for resolving conflicts, problem-solving techniques, and the avoidance of needless conflicts. Coping strategies are also ways of approaching tasks, setting priorities, and determining what one can live with and what one can live without.

2. Options During Problem-Solving

Options are all the ways to solve a problem. Even very capable adults often talk over a problem with another adult just in order to see other options they haven't considered.

3. Information and Know-How

This is a key aspect of a support system. When a child has homework, who in the support system knows enough math to help the child? Who knows the research process? Who knows the ropes for going to college or getting a new-car loan? Who knows how to talk to the insurance agent so the situation can be clarified? Who knows how to negotiate difficult situations with a teacher and come to a resolution? Who understands the court system, the school system? Information and know-how are crucial to success.

4. Temporary Relief from Emotional, Mental, Financial, and/or Time Constraints

When you are upset, who provides relief for you? When you aren't sure how you will get everything finished, who helps you? Who takes your children when you are desperate for a break? These people are all part of a support system.

5. Connections to Other People and Resources

When you don't have the information and know-how, who are the people you turn to for assistance? Those people are your connections. Connections to people and resources are an integral part of a healthy support system.

6. Positive Self-Talk

Everyone has a little voice inside his/her head that talks to him/her all the time. This little voice gives encouraging messages. These encouraging messages help one finish tasks, complete projects, and get through difficult situations. If an individual does not listen to this encouraging little voice, the success rate is much lower.

7. Procedural Self-Talk

Procedural self-talk is the voice that talks an individual through a task. It is key to success. Many individuals in poverty have a very limited support system—and particularly missing is procedural self-talk. Many tasks are never finished. In numerous dealings with students, teachers and other school officials find that self-talk is simply not available to the student.

The following case study identifies what aspects of a support system would be beneficial to a student—and would promote success.

LAKEITHA

You are a high school social studies teacher in inner-city Houston. One of your students, LaKeitha, was so rude in your 10th-grade class that you told her she could not return until you had a conversation with her mother. She calls her mother and tells you that her mom will be there at 7:30 a.m. the next day to meet with you. You are at school the next morning at 7:15 a.m. LaKeitha's mother doesn't show up.

The next day LaKeitha is waiting for you before school. She is crying. She apologizes profusely for her behavior in class and tells you the following: Her dad is in jail. She is the oldest of five children. Her mother works two jobs, and LaKeitha works from 5:00 to 9:00 p.m. at Burger King every day to bring in money. Yesterday her mother was on her way to school to see you, but she got stopped by the police for an expired inspection sticker. Because she didn't have a driver's license, she was put in jail. Her mother is still in jail, and LaKeitha is all alone with the children. She is 15 years old.

LaKeitha asks to be allowed back into your class, and she asks you to help get her mother out of jail.

WHAT SUPPORT SYSTEMS CAN BE ACCESSED TO HELP LAKEITHA?

Here is a sample list of the support systems some schools use to help students.

Support Systems Schools Use

1. *Schoolwide homework support:* A very successful middle school in Texas schedules the last 45 minutes of every day for homework support. Students who did not get their homework done must go to the cafeteria where tutors are available to help them with their homework. The students must stay until their homework is finished. School officials have arranged for a late bus run to take students home. Many poor students do not have access to adults who have the knowledge base to help them with homework. The school has built this into the school day. Another middle school

has arranged for students to have two sets of textbooks—one set at home and one at school. This school does not have lockers. The school has eliminated several problems and has also provided support for students.

2. *Supplemental schoolwide reading programs:* Many schools have gone to the concept of an Accelerated Reader program, using a computer-based management program that provides tests for students to take over the book(s) they have read. Students are encouraged to read more because the programs are designed so that students aren't penalized for what their parents don't know or cannot provide for them.

3. *Keeping students with the same teacher(s) for two or more years or having a school within a school* are other options. Both of these concepts are designed to build longer-term relationships between teachers and students. Also, much less time is wasted at the beginning of the year establishing relationships with the students and their parents.

4. *Teaching coping strategies* can be done in several ways. One is to address each issue as a student needs assistance. Many schools have small groups that meet with the counselor, principal, or a teacher during lunch to work on coping strategies in a number of areas. This ongoing group support allows students to discuss issues and ways to deal with those issues. For example, one elementary school divided all of its sixth-graders into groups of eight. Then school officials took these students and met with them for four weeks, twice a week over lunch, to discuss the issues they would face the next year when they went on to junior high school. Another school has a similar group of students meet who are physically aggressive; the discussion centers around ways to lessen the aggression at school. Advisory groups are yet another way to address issues of support.

5. *Schoolwide scheduling* that puts students in subgroups by skill for reading and math can be a way of providing support. One concern with heterogeneous grouping is the difficulty for the teacher to address all of the diverse instructional needs in the classroom simultaneously. One elementary school scheduled the hour for math at the same time in grades 1 through 3, as well as 4 through 6. Students were then pretested and moved to the appropriate group for that particular unit of instruction. Within two years, the math scores in that building made a considerable gain.

6. *Parent training and contact through video* is invaluable, particularly in poor communities. One pattern in poor communities is that virtually everyone has a VCR or DVD player because of the value placed on entertainment. A principal in Illinois who had 95% of his parents on welfare started a very successful program of parental education and contact through videos. Each teacher in the building made a 15-minute videotape. During that 15 minutes, the teacher made a personal introduction, gave an overview of the instruction for the year, identified the expectations of the class, and encouraged the parents to visit or call. Five copies of each video were made and during the first month of school each student could take a copy home and have an adult view the video. This was very successful for several reasons: (1) Parents who were not literate could understand, (2) it provided a kinesthetic view and feel for what kind of teacher the child had, (3) the parent was not dependent on transportation to have a contact with the school, and (4) it prevented unnecessary miscommunications early in the year. It is a low-cost intervention, and other short videos could be made for parents about school rules, appropriate discipline, etc.

7. *The direct-teaching of classroom survival skills* makes a difference, according to the research. What are classroom survival skills?

Many of these skills are referred to as study skills, but there are also the cognitive strategies that are discussed in Chapter 8 on Instruction. These include such simple hidden rules as how to stay in your seat, how to participate appropriately, where to put your things, etc.

8. *Requiring daily goal-setting and procedural self-talk* would move many of these students light years ahead. In the beginning, goal-setting would focus on what a student wants to accomplish by the end of each day and by the end of the week. Goals would be in writing. At the end of the day, five minutes would need to be taken with the class to see if the goals were met or not. Procedural self-talk would begin in the written form; most students likely would need assistance. Procedural self-talk has value only when tied to a specific task. Procedures vary with tasks.

9. *Team interventions* are a way to provide support to students. This happens when all the teachers of a student meet with the parent(s) to make a plan for helping that student be more successful. This works as long as the intervention with the parent(s) is positive and supportive.

DEBRIEFING THE LAKEITHA CASE STUDY

One of LaKeitha's issues is simply time. She doesn't have any extra time. One of the things the teacher can have LaKeitha do is identify when, given her schedule, she can get things done. The teacher needs to provide flexibility for her to finish her assignments (maybe an extra day) and be flexible about the interruptions that will be a part of her life. The teacher can also give LaKeitha phone numbers and addresses of organizations (churches, social agencies, etc.) that can help provide some relief to her—mentally, emotionally, financially, and physically. Someone needs to spend five minutes with LaKeitha explaining how to access the adult voice, and how using that voice will help her negotiate her difficulties with authority figures and be a better caretaker of her siblings. Certainly of great importance is the acceptance and understanding of her situation by the teacher.

WHAT DOES THIS INFORMATION MEAN IN THE SCHOOL OR WORK SETTING?

■ By reorganizing the school day and schedule, and often by making minor adjustments, educators can build support systems into the school day without additional cost.

■ Support systems need to include the teaching of procedural self-talk, positive self-talk, planning, goal-setting, coping strategies, appropriate relationships, options during problem-solving, access to information and know-how, and connections to additional resources.

CHAPTER 7

Discipline

I n poverty, discipline is about penance and forgiveness, not necessarily change. Because love is unconditional and because the time frame is the present, the notion that discipline should be instructive and change behavior is not part of the culture in generational poverty. In matriarchal, generational poverty, the mother has the most powerful position and is, in some ways, "keeper of the soul." So she dispenses the judgments, determines the amount and price of penance, and offers forgiveness. When forgiveness is granted, behaviors and activities return to the way they were before the incident.

It is important to note that the approach to discipline advocated in this book is to teach a separate set of behaviors. Many of the behaviors that students bring to school are necessary to help them survive outside of school. Just as students learn to use various rules, depending on the computer game they're playing, they also need to learn to use certain rules to be successful in school settings and circumstances. If students from poverty don't know how to fight physically, they are going to be in danger on the streets. But if that is their only method for resolving a problem, then they cannot be successful in school.

The culture of poverty does not provide for success in middle class because middle class to a large extent requires the self-governance of behavior. To be successful in work and in school requires self-control concerning behavior. What, then, do schools need to do to teach appropriate behavior?

STRUCTURE AND CHOICE

The two anchors of any effective discipline program that moves students to self-governance are structure and choice. The program must clearly delineate the expected behaviors and the probable consequences of not choosing those behaviors. The program must also emphasize that the individual always has a choice—to follow or not to follow the expected behaviors. With each choice then comes a consequence—either desirable or not desirable. Many discipline workshops use this approach and are available to schools.

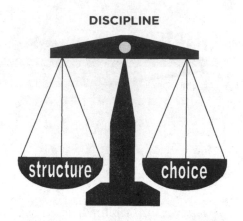

When the focus is "I'll tell you what to do and when," the student is unable to move from dependence to independence, remaining at the level of dependence.

BEHAVIOR ANALYSIS

Mentally, or in writing, the educator is advised to first answer certain questions about the behavior. When these questions are answered, they lead to the strategies that will most help the student.

BEHAVIOR ANALYSIS

1. What kinds of behaviors does a child need to be successful?

2. Does the child have the resources to develop those behaviors?

3. Will it help to contact parent(s)?
   Are resources available through them?
   What resources are available through the school/district

4. How will behaviors be taught?

5. What are other choices the child could make?

6. What will help the child repeat the successful behavior?

The following chart indicates possible explanations of behaviors, along with suggested interventions.

BEHAVIOR RELATED TO POVERTY	INTERVENTION
LAUGH WHEN DISCIPLINED: A way to save face in matriarchal poverty.	Understand the reason for the behavior. Tell students three or four other behaviors that would be more appropriate.
ARGUE LOUDLY WITH THE TEACHER: Poverty is participatory, and the culture has a distrust of authority. See the system as inherently dishonest and unfair.	Don't argue with students. Use the four-part sheet later in this chapter and have students write the answers to the questions. Model respect for students.
ANGRY RESPONSE: Anger is based on fear. Question what the fear is: loss of face?	Respond in the adult voice. When students cool down, discuss other responses they could have used.
INAPPROPRIATE OR VULGAR COMMENTS: Reliance on casual register; may not know formal register.	Have students generate (or teach students other) phrases that could be used to say the same thing.
PHYSICALLY FIGHT: Necessary to survive in poverty. Only know the language of survival. Do not have language or belief system to use conflict resolution. See themselves as less than a man or woman if they don't fight.	Stress that fighting is unacceptable in school. Examine other options that students could live with at school other than fighting. One option is not to settle the business at school, for example.
HANDS ALWAYS ON SOMEONE ELSE: Poverty has a heavy reliance on non-verbal data and touch.	Allow them to draw or doodle. Have them hold their hands behind their back when in line or standing. Give them as much to do with their hands as is possible in a constructive way.
CANNOT FOLLOW DIRECTIONS: Little procedural memory used in poverty. Sequence not used or valued.	Write steps on the board. Have them write at the top of the paper the steps needed to finish the task. Have them practice procedural self-talk.

continued on next page

BEHAVIOR RELATED TO POVERTY	INTERVENTION
EXTREMELY DISORGANIZED: Lack of planning, scheduling, or prioritizing skills. Not taught in poverty. Also, probably don't have a place at home to put things so that they can be found.	Teach a simple, color-coded method of organization in the classroom. Use the five-finger method for memory at the end of the day. Have each student give a plan for organization.
COMPLETE ONLY PART OF A TASK: No procedural self-talk. Do not "see" the whole task.	Write on the board all the parts of the task. Require each student to check off each part when finished.
DISRESPECTFUL TO TEACHER: Have a lack of respect for authority and the system. May not know any adults worthy of respect.	Tell students that disrespect is not a choice. Identify for students the correct voice tone and word choice that are acceptable. This allows students to practice.
HARM OTHER STUDENTS, VERBALLY OR PHYSICALLY: This may be a way of life. Probably a way to buy space or distance. May have become a habitual response. Poverty tends to address issues in the negative.	Tell students that aggression is not a choice. Have students generate other options that are appropriate choices at school. Give students phrases that can be used instead of the one(s) used.
CHEAT OR STEAL: Indicative of weak support system, weak role models/ emotional resources. May indicate extreme financial need. May indicate little instruction/guidance during formative years.	Use a metaphor story (see example later in this chapter) to find the reason or need behind the cheating or stealing. Address the reason or need. Emphasize that the behavior is illegal and not an option at school.
TALK INCESSANTLY: Poverty is very participatory.	Have students write all questions and responses on a notecard two days a week. Tell students that each gets five comments a day. Build participatory activities into the lesson.

PARTICIPATION OF THE STUDENT

While the teacher or administrator is analyzing, the student must analyze as well. To help the student do so, this four-part questionnaire is given to the student for completion. This has been used with students as young as second semester of first grade. Children in poverty have the most difficulty with Question #3. Basically, they see no other choices available than the one they have made.

In going over the sheet with the student, the educator is urged to discuss other choices that could have been made. Students often know only one choice. They don't have access to another way to deal with the situation. For example, if I slam my finger in the car door, I can cry, cuss, hit the car, be silent, kick the tire, laugh, stoically open the car door, groan, etc. I have a wide variety of choices.

NAME: _____

1. What did you do? _____

2. When you did that, what did you want? _____

3. List four other things you could have done.

   1. _____

   2. _____

   3. _____

   4. _____

4. What will you do next time? _____

THE LANGUAGE OF NEGOTIATION

One of the biggest issues with students from poverty is the fact that many children in poverty must function as their own parents. They parent themselves and others—often younger siblings. In many instances they also act as parent to the adult in the household.

Inside virtually everyone's head are three internal voices that guide the individual. These voices are the child voice, the adult voice, and the parent voice. It has been my observation that individuals who have become their own parent quite young do not have an internal adult voice. They have a child voice and a parent voice, but not an adult voice.

An internal adult voice allows for negotiation. This voice provides the language of negotiation and allows issues to be examined in a non-threatening way.

Educators tend to speak to students in a parent voice, particularly in discipline situations. To the student who is already functioning as a parent, this is unbearable. Almost immediately, the situation is exacerbated beyond the original incident. The tendency for educators to use the parent voice with students who are poor is based on the assumption that a lack of resources must indicate a lack of intelligence. Students and parents in poverty are very offended by this.

When the parent voice is used with a student who is already a parent in many ways, the outcome is anger. The student is angry because anger is based on fear. What the parent voice forces the student to do is use either the child voice or the parent voice. If the student uses the parent voice, which could sound sarcastic in this context, the student will get in trouble. If the student uses the child voice, he/she will feel helpless and therefore at the mercy of the adult. Many students choose to use the parent voice because it is less frightening than memories connected with being helpless.

Part of the reality of poverty is the language of survival. There are simply not enough resources for people in poverty to engage in a discussion of them. For example, if there are five hot dogs and five people, the distribution of the food is fairly clear. The condiments for the hot dogs are going to be limited, so the discussion about their distribution will be fairly limited as well. Contrast that, for example, with a middle-class household where the discussion will be about how many hot dogs, what should go on the hot dog, how much of each ingredient, etc. Thus the ability to see options and to negotiate among those options is not well developed.

To teach students to use the "language of negotiation" one must first teach them the phrases they can use. Especially beginning in fourth grade, have them use the "adult" voice in discussions. Direct-teach the notion of an adult voice, and give them phrases to use. Have them tally each time they use a phrase from the "adult" voice. There will be laughter. However, over time, if the teacher also models that voice in interactions with students, one will hear more of those kinds of questions and statements.

In addition to this strategy, several staff-development programs are available to teach peer negotiation. It is important that, as part of the negotiation, the culture of origin is not denigrated, but rather the ability to negotiate is seen as a survival tool for the work and school setting.

THREE VOICES

Adapted from the work of Eric Berne

THE CHILD VOICE *
Defensive, victimized, emotional, whining, losing attitude, strongly negative non-verbal.

- Quit picking on me.
- You don't love me.
- You want me to leave.
- Nobody likes (loves) me.
- I hate you.
- You're ugly.

- You make me sick.
- It's your fault.
- Don't blame me.
- She, he, _____ did it.
- You make me mad.
- You made me do it.

* *The child voice is also playful, spontaneous, curious, etc. The phrases listed often occur in conflictual or manipulative situations and impede resolution.*

THE PARENT VOICE * **
Authoritative, directive, judgmental, evaluative, win-lose mentality, demanding, punitive, sometimes threatening.

- You shouldn't (should) do that.

- It's wrong (right) to do _____ .

- That's stupid, immature, out of line, ridiculous.

- Life's not fair. Get busy.

- You are good, bad, worthless, beautiful (any judgmental, evaluative comment).

- You do as I say.

- If you weren't so _____ , this wouldn't happen to you.

- Why can't you be like _____ ?

* *The parent voice can also be very loving and supportive. The phrases listed usually occur during conflict and impede resolution.*

** *The internal parent voice can create shame and guilt.*

THE ADULT VOICE
Non-judgmental, free of negative non-verbal, factual, often in question format, attitude of win-win.

- In what ways could this be resolved?

- What factors will be used to determine the effectiveness, quality of _____ ?

- I would like to recommend _____ .

- What are choices in this situation?

- I am comfortable (uncomfortable) with _____ .

- Options that could be considered are _____ .

- For me to be comfortable, I need the following things to occur
  _____ .

- These are the consequences of that choice/action _____ .

- We agree to disagree.

USING METAPHOR STORIES

Another technique for working with students and adults is to use a metaphor story. A metaphor story will help an individual voice issues that affect subsequent actions. A metaphor story does not have any proper names in it and goes like this.

A student keeps going to the nurse's office two or three times a week. There is nothing wrong with her. Yet she keeps going. Adult says to Jennifer, the girl, "Jennifer, I am going to tell a story and I need you to help me. It's about a fourth-grade girl much like yourself. I need you to help me tell the story because I'm not in fourth grade.

"Once upon a time there was a girl who went to the nurse's office. Why did the girl go to the nurse's office? (*Because she thought there was something wrong with her.*) So the girl went to the nurse's office because she thought there was something wrong with her. Did the nurse find anything wrong with her? (*No, the nurse did not.*) So the nurse did not find anything wrong with her, yet the girl kept going to the nurse. Why did the girl keep going to the nurse? (*Because she thought there was something wrong with her.*) So the girl thought something was wrong with her. Why did the girl think there was something wrong with her? (*She saw a TV show . . .*)"

The story continues until the reason for the behavior is found, and then the story needs to end on a positive note. "So she went to the doctor, and he gave her tests and found that she was OK."

This is an actual case. What came out in the story was that Jennifer had seen a TV show in which a girl her age had died suddenly and had never known she was ill. Jennifer's parents took her to the doctor, he ran tests, and he told her she was fine. So she didn't go to the nurse's office anymore.

A metaphor story is to be used one on one when there is a need to understand the existing behavior and motivate the student to implement the appropriate behavior.

TEACHING HIDDEN RULES

For example, if a student from poverty laughs when he/she is disciplined, the teacher needs to say, "Do you use the same rules to play all computer games? No, you don't because you would lose. The same is true at school. There are street rules and there are school rules. Each set of rules helps you be successful where you are. So, at school, laughing when being disciplined is not a choice. It doesn't help you be successful. It only buys you more trouble. Keep a straight face and look sorry, even if you don't feel that way."

This is an example of teaching a hidden rule. It can be even more straightforward with older students. "Look, there are hidden rules on the streets and hidden rules at school. What are they?"

After the discussion, detail the rules that make students successful where they are.

WHAT DOES THIS INFORMATION MEAN IN THE SCHOOL OR WORK SETTING?

■ Students from poverty need to have at least two sets of behaviors from which to choose—one for the street and one for the school and work settings.

■ The purpose of discipline should be to promote successful behaviors at school.

■ Teaching students to use the adult voice (i.e., the language of negotiation) is important for success in and out of school and can become an alternative to physical aggression.

■ Structure and choice need to be part of the discipline approach.

■ Discipline should be seen and used as a form of instruction.

CHAPTER 8

Instruction and Improving Achievement

One of the overriding purposes of this book is to improve the achievement of students from poverty. *Low achievement is closely correlated with lack of resources, and numerous studies have documented the correlation between low socioeconomic status and low achievement* (Hodgkinson, 1995). To improve achievement, however, we will need to rethink our instruction and instructional arrangements.

TRADITIONAL NOTIONS OF INTELLIGENCE

For years, and still very prevalent, is the notion that nearly all intelligence is inherited. In fact, the book *The Bell Curve* purports that individuals in poverty have on the average an IQ of nine points lower than individuals in the middle class. That might be a credible argument if IQ tests really measure ability. What IQ tests measure is acquired information. Try the following IQ test and see how you do.

IQ TEST

1. What is *gray tape* and what is it used for?

2. What does *dissed* mean?

3. What are the *advantages* and *disadvantages* of moving often?

4. What is the *main* kind of *work* that a *bondsman* does?

5. What is a *roach*?

6. How are a *pawnshop* and a *convenience store* alike? How are they different?

7. Why is it important for a non–U.S. citizen to have a *green card*?

8. You go to the bakery store. You can buy five loaves of day-old bread for 39 cents each or seven loaves of three-day-old bread for 28 cents each. Which choice will cost less?

9. What does *deportation* mean?

10. What is the difference between *marriage* and a *common law* relationship?

These questions are representative of the kinds of questions that are asked on IQ tests. This test is only different in one way: the content. Yet it illustrates clearly the point that the information tested on many IQ tests is only acquired knowledge. IQ tests were designed to predict success in school. However, they do not predict ability or basic intelligence. If middle-class students were to take this (invalidated) test, they could possibly have nine IQ points fewer than many students in poverty. Therefore, the assessments and tests we use in many areas of school are not about ability or intelligence. They are about an acquired knowledge base; if your parents are educated, chances are you will have a higher acquired knowledge base. A better approach to achievement is to look at teaching and learning.

DIFFERENTIATING BETWEEN TEACHING AND LEARNING

The emphasis since 1980 in education has been on teaching. The theory has been that if you teach well enough, then learning will occur. But we all know of situations and individuals, including ourselves, who decided in a given situation not to learn. And we have all been in situations where we found it virtually impossible to learn because we did not have the background information or the belief system to accept it, even though it was well-taught and presented.

> Teaching is what occurs outside the head.
> Learning is what occurs inside the head.

In order to learn, an individual must have certain cognitive skills and must have a structure inside his/her head to accept the learning—a file cabinet or a piece of software. Traditionally, we have given the research on teaching to teachers and the research on learning to counselors and early-childhood teachers. It is the research on learning that must be addressed if we are to work successfully with students from poverty.

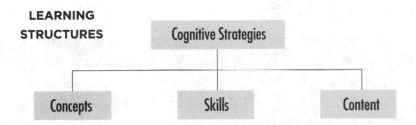

In this oversimplified representation of a learning structure are four elements. The first is *Cognitive Strategies*. These are even more basic than concepts. They are fundamental ways of processing information. They are the infrastructure of the mind. *Concepts* store information and allow for retrieval. *Skills*—i.e., reading, writing, computing, language—comprise the processing of content. *Content* is the "what" of learning—the information used to make sense of daily life. Traditionally in schools we have assumed that the cognitive strategies are in place. If they are not, we test and place the student in a special program: special education, dyslexia, Chapter 1, ADHD, 504, etc. Little attempt is made to address the cognitive strategies because we believe that to a large extent they are not remediable. We focus our efforts in pre-K and K on building concepts. We devote first through third grades to building skills. We enhance those skills in grades 4 and 5. And when the student gets into sixth grade, and on to 12th grade, we teach content.

The truth is that we can no longer pretend this arrangement works—no matter how well or how hard we teach. Increasingly, students, mostly from poverty, are coming to school without the concepts, but more importantly, without the cognitive strategies. We simply can't assign them all to special education. What are these cognitive strategies, and how do we build learning structures inside the heads of students?

COGNITIVE STRATEGIES

Compelling work in this area has been done by Reuven Feuerstein, an Israeli. He began in 1945 working with poor, disenfranchised Jewish youths who settled in Israel after World War II. He had studied under Jean Piaget and disagreed with Piaget in one major way. He felt that between the environmental stimulus and the response should be mediation (i.e., the intervention of an adult).

MEDIATION		
Identification of the STIMULUS	Assignment of MEANING	Identification of a STRATEGY

Mediation is basically three things: identification of the stimulus, assignment of meaning, and identification of a strategy. For example, we say to a child, "Don't cross the street. You could get hit by a car. So if you must cross the street, look both ways twice."

WHY IS MEDIATION SO IMPORTANT?

Mediation builds cognitive strategies, and those strategies give individuals the ability to plan, systematically go through data, etc.

If an individual depends upon a random, episodic story structure for memory patterns, lives in an unpredictable environment, and *has not developed the ability to plan,* then . . .

If an individual cannot plan, he/she *cannot predict.*

If an individual cannot predict, he/she *cannot identify cause and effect.*

If an individual cannot identify cause and effect, he/she *cannot identify consequence.*

If an individual cannot identify consequence, he/she *cannot control impulsivity.*

If an individual cannot control impulsivity, he/she *has an inclination toward criminal behavior.*

Feuerstein identified the missing links that occur in the mind when mediation had not occurred. These students by any standard would have been identified as special-education students. Yet, with his program, many of these students who came to him in the mid-teens went on to be very successful, with some even completing Ph.D.s. To teach these strategies, Feuerstein developed more than 50 instruments. What are these missing cognitive strategies?

MISSING LINKS

(Feuerstein, 1980; Sharron, 1994):

1. *"Mediated focusing"*— Ability to focus attention and see objects in detail. Opposite of blurred and sweeping perceptions.

2. *"Mediated scheduling"*— Based on routine. Ability to schedule and plan ahead. Ability to represent the future abstractly and therefore set goals.

3. *"Mediation of positive anticipation"*— Ability to control the present for a happy representation of the future.

4. *"Mediation of inhibition and control"*— Ability to defer gratification, think before acting, control impulsiveness.

5. *"Mediated representation of the future"*— Ability to construe imaginatively a future scenario based on facts.

6. *"Mediation of verbal stimulation"*— Use of precise language for defining and categorizing the environment.

7. *"Mediated precision"*— Ability to precisely define situations, things, people, etc., and use that precise thinking for problem-solving.

Missing links/mediations result in cognitive issues.

What Are These Cognitive Issues?

Blurred and sweeping perceptions and the lack of a systematic method of exploration mean that these students have no consistent or predictable way of getting information. They see only about 50% of what is on a page. If you watch these students in a new setting, they will rapidly go from object to object, touching everything. Yet when you ask them what they have seen, they cannot tell you. This area is related to the use of the casual-register story structure, which is episodic and random in the details or information presented. They simply do not have cognitive methodology for doing tasks or a systematic way to finish tasks.

Impaired verbal tools means they do not have the vocabulary to deal with the cognitive tasks. Vocabulary words are the building blocks of the internal learning structure. Vocabulary is also the tool to better define a problem, seek more accurate solutions, etc. Many students who rely solely on casual register do not use or have many prepositions or adverbs in their speech.

Impaired spatial orientation is simply the inability to orient objects, people, etc., in space. Directions, location, object size, object shape, etc., are not available to them. They have neither the vocabulary nor the concepts for spatial orientation.

Impaired temporal orientation is the inability to organize and measure in time. One of Feuerstein's observations was that these students assign time to incidents on the basis of the emotional intensity of the experience, not the measured time that is part of educated thinking. I find among students from poverty that time is neither measured nor heeded. Being somewhere on time is seldom valued. And time itself is not seen as a thing to be used or valued.

Impaired observations of constancies is the inability of the brain to hold an object inside the head and keep the memory of the object constant. In other words, when there are impaired observations of constancies, objects change shape and size in the mind. If this is the case, then learning alphabet letters, retaining shapes, etc., are problematic. It is also the inability to know what stays the same and what changes. For example, east and west are always constant; left and right change based on the orientation of the moment.

Lack of precision and accuracy in data-gathering is another cognitive issue. It is related to several of the above issues. Problem-solving and other tasks are extremely problematic because students from poverty seldom have the strategies to gather precise and accurate data.

Another cognitive issue is the inability *to hold two objects or two sources inside the head while comparing and contrasting*. If a student is unable to do this, he/she cannot assign information to categories inside his/her brain. If a student cannot assign information to categories, then he/she cannot retrieve the information except in an associative, random way.

These issues explain many of the student behaviors. How do we make interventions?

What Are These Cognitive Strategies That Must Be Built?

Feuerstein identified three stages in the learning process: "input, elaboration, and output."

1. Input Strategies

Input is defined as "quantity and quality of the data gathered."

1. Use planning behaviors.

2. Focus perception on specific stimulus.

3. Control impulsivity.

4. Explore data systematically.

5. Use appropriate and accurate labels.

6. Organize space with stable systems of reference.

7. Orient data in time.

8. Identify constancies across variations.

9. Gather precise and accurate data.

10. Consider two sources of information at once.

11. Organize data (parts of a whole).

12. Visually transport data.

2. Elaboration Strategies

Elaboration is defined as "use of the data."

1. Identify and define the problem.

2. Select relevant cues.

3. Compare data.

4. Select appropriate categories of time.

5. Summarize data.

6. Project relationships of data.

7. Use logical data.

8. Test hypothesis.

9. Build inferences.

10. Make a plan using the data.

11. Use appropriate labels.

12. Use data systematically.

3. Output Strategies

Ouput is defined as "communication of the data."

1. Communicate clearly the labels and process.

2. Visually transport data correctly.

3. Use precise and accurate language.

4. Control impulsive behavior.

What do these strategies mean?

Mediation builds these strategies. When these strategies are not present, they can be built. Typically in school, we begin teaching at the elaboration level (i.e., use of the data). When students do not understand, we reteach these strategies, but we do not revisit the quality and quantity of the data gathered.

Input Strategies (Quality and Quantity of Data)

Use planning behaviors includes goal-setting, identifying the procedures in the task, identifying the parts of the task, assigning time to the task(s), and identifying the quality of the work necessary to complete the task.

Focus perception on specific stimulus is the strategy of seeing every detail on the page or in the environment. It is the strategy of identifying everything noticed by the five senses.

Control impulsivity is the strategy of stopping action until one has thought about the task. There is a direct correlation between impulse control and improved behavior and achievement.

Explore data systematically means that a strategy is employed to procedurally and systematically go through every piece of data. Numbering is a way to go systematically through data. Highlighting each piece of data can be another method.

Use appropriate and accurate labels is the use of precise words and vocabulary to identify and explain. If a student does not have specific words to use, then his/her ability to retrieve and use information is severely limited. It is not enough that a student can do a task, he/she must also be able to label the procedures, tasks, and processes so that the task can be successfully repeated each time and analyzed at a metacognitive level. Metacognition is the ability to think about one's thinking. To do so, labels must be attached. Only when labels are attached can the task be evaluated and, therefore, improved.

Organize space with stable systems of reference is crucial to success in math. It means that up, down, right, left, across, horizontal, vertical, diagonal, etc., are understood. It means that an individual can identify with labels the position of an item. It means that a person can organize space. For example, if an individual doesn't have this strategy, then it's virtually impossible to tell p, b, and d apart. The only differentiation is the orientation in space.

Orient data in time is the strategy of assigning abstract values to time and the measurement of time. This strategy is crucial for identifying cause and effect, for determining sequence, and for predicting consequences.

Identify constancies across variations is the strategy of knowing what always remains the same and what changes. For example, if you do not know what always makes a square a square, you cannot identify constancies. It allows one to define things, to recognize a person or an object, and to compare and contrast. This strategy allows cursive writing to be read in all of its variations. I once asked a group of fifth-grade students I was working with this question: "If you saw me tomorrow, what about me would be the same and what would be different?" Many of the students had difficulty with that concept.

Gather precise and accurate data is the strategy of using accurate labels, identifying the orientation in time and space, knowing the constancies, and exploring the data systematically.

Consider two sources of information at once is the strategy of visually transporting data accurately, identifying the constancies and variations, and exploring the data systematically. When that is done, then precise and accurate labels need to be assigned.

Organize data (*parts of a whole*) involves exploring data systematically, organizing space, identifying constancies and variations, and labeling the parts and the whole with precise words.

Visually transport data is when the eye picks up the data, carries it accurately to the brain, examines it for constancies and variations, and labels the parts and the whole.

Elaboration and Output Strategies

These tend to be fairly well understood in schools because that is where the teaching tends to occur.

WHAT WOULD LESSON DESIGN LOOK LIKE WHEN THESE STRATEGIES ARE TAUGHT?

The lesson would center around what the student would do. Sometime during the lesson students would need to exhibit these five skills:

THE STUDENT WOULD:	
	Use planning behaviors.
	Control impulsivity.
	Use evaluative behaviors.
	Explore data systematically.
	Use specific language.

Regardless of content, if the lesson requires that in some way students do these five things, cognitive strategies would be strengthened, discipline would improve, and achievement would be enhanced.

USING EYE MOVEMENT TO FOLLOW THE LEARNING AND PROCESSING

Bandler and Grinder (1979) did a great deal of work with non-verbal cues and cognitive processing. This work is known as neuro-linguistic programming. But of particular interest to educators is the work on eye movement because it allows a teacher to begin understanding the way(s) in which a student is processing information. Criminologists use these techniques to break crimes, lawyers use them to cross-examine witnesses, and salespeople use them to enhance sales. *Influencing with Integrity* by Laborde (1983) is a layperson's explanation of the information. Briefly, however, the main concepts will be explained.

Think of the human face as a clock. It is as you look at the face. To begin, the face has three zones. When a person's gaze is directed in the top zone, the individual is processing visual information. When eyes are in the middle zone, the individual is processing auditory information (with one exception).

When eyes are in the bottom zone, the individual is either talking to himself/herself or processing feelings.

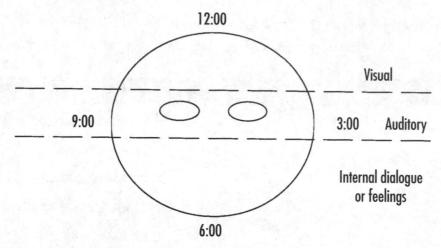

VISUAL

Now let's go to the next level of information. If the person being observed is right-handed, then the 2 o'clock position indicates that the individual is processing visually remembered data. Around 10 o'clock the individual is processing data that are visually constructed. In other words, the individual is putting together data from several sources. If the person is left-handed, then 2 o'clock is visually constructed, and 10 o'clock is visually remembered.

AUDITORY

If the person is right-handed, the 3 o'clock position indicates auditory remembered and 9 o'clock position indicates auditory constructed. If the individual is left-handed, then 3 o'clock is auditory constructed and 9 o'clock is auditory remembered.

FEELING/KINESTHETIC

If the individual is right-handed, the 5 o'clock position is auditory internal dialogue, and the 7 o'clock position is feelings. If the individual is left-handed, then 5 o'clock is feelings, while 7 o'clock is auditory internal dialogue.

VISUAL CONSTRUCT

If eyes are staring straight ahead and defocused, the individual is in a visual-construct position.

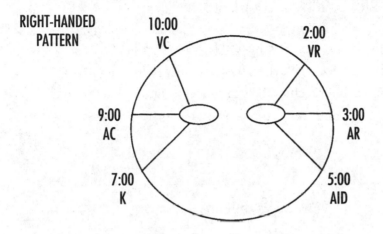

RIGHT-HANDED PATTERN

10:00 VC — 2:00 VR — 9:00 AC — 3:00 AR — 7:00 K — 5:00 AID

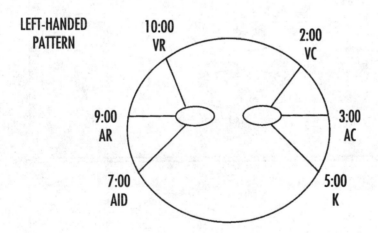

LEFT-HANDED PATTERN

10:00 VR — 2:00 VC — 9:00 AR — 3:00 AC — 7:00 AID — 5:00 K

How does knowing eye movement help a teacher? If a student has moved his/her eyes to a visual position, then the teacher knows that the student is trying to find the information visually. The teacher can enhance the process by asking the student, "What do you see?" If the student is processing from an auditory position, the teacher can ask, "What do you remember hearing?"

And so on for the other positions. Eye movements can help the teacher identify how a student tends to store and retrieve information.

ADDITIONAL INSTRUCTIONAL INTERVENTIONS THAT BUILD CONCEPTUAL FRAMEWORKS AND COGNITIVE STRATEGIES

1. *Using graphic organizers* (Idol and Jones, 1991, Chapter 3). Graphic organizers give students the ability to identify main concepts, assign specific labels to concepts, and sort relevant and non-relevant cues (see example below).

Example:

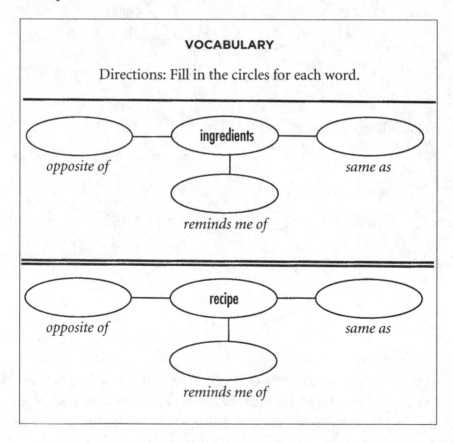

Example:

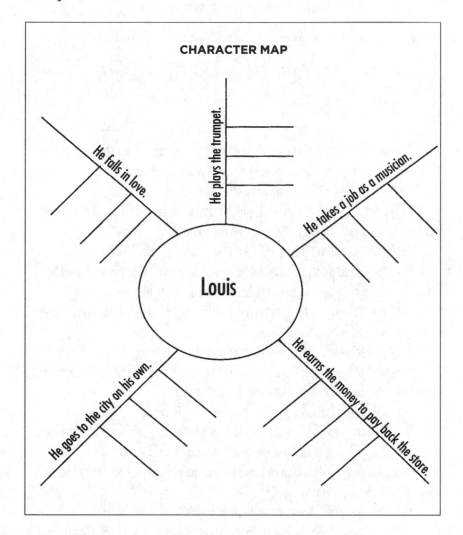

(For a comprehensive, research-based overview, see Idol and Jones, 1991.)

2. *Identifying methods of having a systematic approach to the data/text.* One way to do this is to provide students a systematic method to go through the text. Some teachers have students highlight information. Here is one example:

SELF-QUESTIONING STRATEGIES

Place the following symbols in the text where you find the answers:

☺ =	Who	Y =	Why
➡ =	Where	X =	When
❑ =	What	H =	How

Three little pigs went out into the world. The first little pig met a man carrying straw. The little pig asked, "May I have some straw so I can build a house?"

"Yes," said the man. "You may have some straw."

The first little pig took the straw. He built a straw house. A wolf came along and knocked on the door. "Little pig, little pig, let me come in."

"Not by the hair of my chinny chin chin!" said the little pig.

"Then I'll huff, and I'll puff, and I'll blow your house in," said the wolf. And he huffed. And he puffed. And he blew the house in. And he ate him up.

The second little pig met a man carrying sticks. The little pig asked, "May I have some sticks so I can build a house?"

"Yes," said the man. "You may have some sticks."

The second little pig took the sticks. He built a stick house. A wolf came along and knocked on the door. "Little pig, little pig, let me come in."

"Not by the hair of my chinny chin chin!" said the little pig.

"Then I'll huff, and I'll puff, and I'll blow your house in," said the wolf. And he huffed. And he puffed. And he blew the house in. And he ate him up.

The third little pig met a man carrying bricks. The little pig asked, "May I have some bricks so I can build a house?"

"Yes," said the man. "You may have some bricks."

The third little pig took the bricks. He built a brick house. A wolf came along and knocked on the door. "Little pig, little pig, let me come in."

"Not by the hair of my chinny chin chin!" said the little pig.

"Then I'll huff, and I'll puff, and I'll blow your house in," said the wolf.

And he huffed. And he puffed. And he huffed. And he puffed. He could not blow the brick house in. The wolf was angry. He jumped on the roof. He yelled, "Little pig, I'm coming down the chimney. I'm going to eat you up!"

But the little pig was smart. He was smarter than the wolf. He had a big pot of hot water in the fireplace. The little pig lifted the cover. The wolf fell into the pot. The little pig lived happily ever after in his little brick house.

3. *Establishing goal-setting and procedural self-talk* (Marzano and Arredondo, 1986). These two activities should be part of daily instruction. The procedural self-talk can be written down and eventually will become part of the internal self-talk. Goal-setting addresses several cognitive issues.

4. *Teaching conceptual frameworks as part of the content* (Marzano and Arredondo, 1986). There are many ways to do this. One is by using graphic organizers. Another is to teach content in an associative way (i.e., teaching it in relationship to what students personally have experienced, rather than in a linear or hierarchical way). Another way to build conceptual frameworks is to take what they know and translate it into the new form. For example, have them write in casual register and then translate into formal register. Or, have them rewrite the story in a poverty structure. In other words, it is an opportunity for students to see the same information in more than one structure. In math, students would both draw the problem and do the problem in an equation.

5. *Using a kinesthetic approach* as part of the classroom environment is another intervention. For example, rather than teaching algebra strictly from equations on paper and pencil, the shop teacher and the algebra teacher would design a project that would require students to use algebra to design and complete a metal-working project. The Tech Prep program uses this approach.

6. *Using rubrics* that show the levels of performance so that students can begin to critique their expertise. What a well-written rubric can do for students is to allow them to evaluate their performance and learn how to improve on that performance. It allows students to begin to address the cognitive problem of not being able to plan or schedule. It allows for the cognitive strategy of

future representation to be developed, because students can see ahead of time the consequences of their choices.

7. *Teaching the structure of language.* Project Read is one such intervention and is a multi-sensory approach to teaching reading and writing. The focus is on teaching structure and patterns so that the student can understand the use of language in formal registers. The campuses in Goose Creek Independent School District in Texas that have implemented this program have significantly higher state test scores than those campuses that have not. For more information about Project Read, please call (800) 450-0343.

8. *Teaching students to make questions* (Palincsar and Brown, 1984). There is a significant relationship between the ability to ask a question syntactically and comprehension of the text. To teach students question-making, simply give them the list of question stems on page 105, and then have them use the text to come up with their own questions. Require them to prepare four answer choices as well. Also, one can use the reciprocal teaching methods designed by Palincsar and Brown.

9. *Sorting relevant from irrelevant cues.* Cartooning is a wonderful way to do this. Have students draw, in six frames, the main points of the text or story. See template on page 106.

10. *Teaching mental models.* To store abstract information in the mind, mental models are used. A mental model can be a two-dimensional drawing, a story, a metaphor, or an analogy.

QUESTION-MAKING STEMS

1. From this story/passage, how might _____ be described?

2. Why was _____ ?

3. Why did _____ ?

4. How else might the author have ended the story?

5. How might the story be different if _____ ?

6. (Use the word in a sentence from the story.) In this story, what does _____ mean?

7. What does the author of this article probably believe?

8. How did _____ feel about _____ ?

9. What caused _____ to _____ ?

10. What is _____ ?

11. When _____ happened, why did _____ ?

12. The article/story states that _____ .
    Why is that information important to the reader?

CARTOON CHAPTER

WHAT DOES THE RESEARCH SAY?

**INSISTENCE
EXPECTATIONS
SUPPORT**

If the research had to be summed up in three words, these are the three (at left) that seem to appear repeatedly. Traditionally in schools we have provided insistence, and since the mid-1970s we have added expectations as part of the discussion. It is, however, the notion of support that must be provided to students now.

What is appropriate support? I am not talking about a fuzzy-feel-good notion of support; I am talking about what girders are to a bridge. The supports these students need are cognitive strategies, appropriate relationships, coping strategies, goal-setting opportunities, and appropriate instruction both in content and discipline. *The true discrimination that comes out of poverty is the lack of cognitive strategies. The lack of these unseen attributes handicaps in every aspect of life the individual who does not have them.*

The Virginia State Department of Education (1993) identified the following four responses as being effective in promoting learning for at-risk students: developmental preschool programs, supplemental reading programs, reducing class size, and schoolwide projects in prevention and support. These four responses could allow for relationships, support, insistence, and development of cognitive strategies. A study of low-performance schools (in which some children achieve) looked at the external resources that students bring to the school (Anderson, Hollinger, and Conaty, 1993). What seems to be more important than involvement and coming to school by parents is whether parents provide insistence, expectations, and support at home. Perhaps we need to rethink the focus of parent training.

In conclusion, as we adapt and flex our instruction to meet the needs of these students, cognitive strategies and support need to be integrated with insistence and expectations.

WHAT DOES THIS INFORMATION MEAN IN THE SCHOOL OR WORK SETTING?

- The focus in schools should be on learning.

- Instruction in the cognitive strategies should be a part of the curriculum.

- Staff development should focus on a diagnostic approach rather than a programmatic approach.

- Efforts to promote learning should pay greater heed to what is in the student's head.

- Insistence, expectations, and support need to be guiding lights in our decisions about instruction.

CHAPTER 9

Creating Relationships

Locate a resilient kid and you will also find a caring adult—
or several—who has guided him.

– Invincible Kids, *U.S. News & World Report*

The key to achievement for students from poverty is in creating relationships with them. Because poverty is about relationships as well as entertainment, the most significant motivator for these students is relationships.

The question becomes, How does a formal institution create relationships? Two sources provide some answers to this question. These sources are (1) the recent research in the field of science and (2) the work Stephen Covey has done with personal effectiveness.

Margaret Wheatley, in her book *Leadership and the New Science* (1992), states quite clearly:

> *Scientists in many different disciplines are questioning whether we can adequately explain how the world works by using the machine imagery created in the 17th century, most notably by Sir Isaac Newton. In the machine model, one must understand parts. Things can be taken apart, dissected literally or representationally . . . and then put back together without any significant loss . . . The Newtonian model of the world is characterized by materialism and reductionism—a focus on things rather than relationships . . . The quantum view of reality strikes against most of our notions of reality. Even to scientists, it is admittedly bizarre. But it is a world where* relationship *is the key determiner of what is observed and of*

how particles manifest themselves ... Many scientists now work with the concept of fields—invisible forces that structure space or behavior (pp. 8–13).

Wheatley goes on to say that, in the new science of quantum physics, physical reality is not just tangible, it is also intangible. Fields are invisible, yet:

[They are the] substance of the universe ... In organizations, which is the more important influence on behavior—the system or the individual? The quantum world answered that question: It depends ... What is critical is the relationship created between the person and the setting. That relationship will always be different, will always evoke different potentialities. It all depends on the players and the moment (pp. 34–35).

Teachers and administrators have always known that relationships, often referred to as "politics," make a great deal of difference—sometimes all of the difference—in what could or could not happen in a building. But since 1980 we have concentrated our energies in schools on "achievement" and "effective teaching strategies." We used the Newtonian approach to teaching, dissecting it into parts. Yet the most important part of learning seems to be related to relationship, if we listen to the data and the potent realities in the research emerging from the disciplines of biology and physics.

When students who have been in poverty (and have successfully made it into middle class) are asked how they made the journey, the answer nine times out of 10 has to do with a relationship—a teacher, counselor, or coach who made a suggestion or took an interest in them as individuals.

Covey (1989) uses the notion of an emotional bank account to convey the crucial aspects of relationships. He indicates that in all relationships one makes deposits to and withdrawals from the other individual in that relationship. The chart on the next page lists some of these deposits and withdrawals.

The first step to creating relationships with students and adults is to make the deposits that are the basis of relationships. Relationships always begin as one individual to another. First and foremost in all relationships with students is the relationship between each teacher and student, then between each

DEPOSITS	WITHDRAWALS
Seek first to understand	Seek first to be understood
Keeping promises	Breaking promises
Kindnesses, courtesies	Unkindnesses, discourtesies
Clarifying expectations	Violating expectations
Loyalty to the absent	Disloyalty, duplicity
Apologies	Pride, conceit, arrogance
Open to feedback	Rejecting feedback

Adapted from Stephen Covey, *The Seven Habits of Highly Effective People*

student and each administrator, and finally, among all of the players, including student-to-student relationships.

What, then, is meant by relationship? (Should students become my personal friends? Should I go out with them?) A successful relationship occurs when emotional deposits are made to the student, emotional withdrawals are avoided, and students are respected. Are there boundaries to the relationship? Absolutely—and that is what is meant by clarifying expectations. But to honor students as human beings worthy of respect and care is to establish a relationship that will provide for enhanced learning.

What are the deposits and withdrawals with regard to students and adults from poverty? (See chart on next page.) By understanding deposits that are valued by students from poverty, the relationship is stronger.

How does an organization or school create—and build—relationships? Through support systems, through caring about students, by promoting student achievement, by being role models, by insisting upon successful behaviors for school. *Support systems are simply networks of relationships.*

Will creating healthy relationships with students make all students successful? No. But if we make a difference for 5% more of our students the

DEPOSITS MADE TO INDIVIDUAL IN POVERTY	WITHDRAWALS MADE FROM INDIVIDUAL IN POVERTY
Appreciation for humor and entertainment provided by the individual	Put-downs or sarcasm about the humor or the individual
Acceptance of what the individual cannot say about a person or situation	Insistence and demands for full explanation about a person or situation
Respect for the demands and priorities of relationships	Insistence on the middle-class view of relationships
Using the adult voice	Using the parent voice
Assisting with goal-setting	Telling the individual his/her goals
Identifying options related to available resources	Making judgments on the value and availability of resources
Understanding the importance of personal freedom, speech, and individual personality	Assigning pejorative character traits to the individual

first year and 5% more each year thereafter, we will have progressed considerably from where we are right now.

In the final analysis, as one looks back on a teaching career, it is the relationships one remembers.

WHAT DOES THIS INFORMATION MEAN IN THE SCHOOL OR WORK SETTING?

- For students and adults from poverty, the primary motivation for their success will be in their relationships.

- If your school or work setting presently affords few opportunities for building relationships, find ways to establish natural connections that will enable this vital resource to take root and grow.

Conclusion

One of the topics as yet untouched is the need to grieve and go through the grieving process as one teaches or works with the poor. The Kubler-Ross stages in the grieving process are anger, denial, bargaining, depression, and acceptance. As one meets and works with a particular family or individual, there is such frustration and, ultimately, grieving because many situations are so embedded as to seem hopeless. It's like dealing with the legendary octopus; each time a tentacle is removed, another appears. Particularly for the adults, so many choices have been made that virtually preclude any resolution that would be acceptable from an educated perspective. Yet the role of the educator or social worker or employer is not to save the individual, but rather to offer a support system, role models, and opportunities to learn, which will increase the likelihood of the person's success. Ultimately, the choice always belongs to the individual.

Yet another notion among the middle class and educated is that if the poor had a choice, they would live differently. The financial resources would certainly help make a difference. Even with the financial resources, however, not every individual who received those finances would choose to live differently. There is a freedom of verbal expression, an appreciation of individual personality, a heightened and intense emotional experience, and a sensual, kinesthetic approach to life usually not found in the middle class or among the educated. These patterns are so intertwined in the daily life of the poor that to have those cut off would be to lose a limb. Many choose not to live a different life. And for some, alcoholism, laziness, lack of motivation, drug addiction, etc., in effect make the choices for the individual.

But it is the responsibility of educators and others who work with the poor to teach the differences and skills/rules that will allow the individual to make the choice. As it now stands for many of the poor, the choice never exists.

Poverty Rates for Children Under 5 by Living Arrangement: 2006

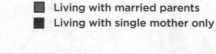

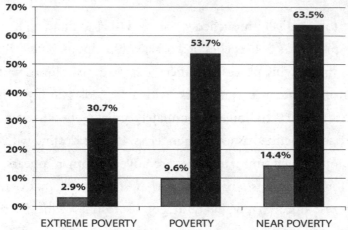

Source: U.S. Census Bureau and Bureau of Labor Statistics,
2007 Current Population Survey

Household Income in 20% Increments of Total: 2006

Group	Average Household Income Ranges: 2006
Lowest 20%	$0 – $19,178
Second 20%	$19,179 – $36,000
Third 20%	$36,001 – $57,658
Fourth 20%	$57,659 – $91,705
Highest 20%	$91,706+
Top 5% (part of highest 20%)	$166,000+

Source: U.S. Census Bureau and Bureau of Labor Statistics,
2007 Annual Demographic Survey

NOTE: The U.S. Census Bureau publishes income and poverty data each year for the previous calendar year. For the most current information provided in this format, visit www.ahaprocess.com.

U.S. Median Income for Persons 25 and Older, by Sex and Educational Attainment: 2006

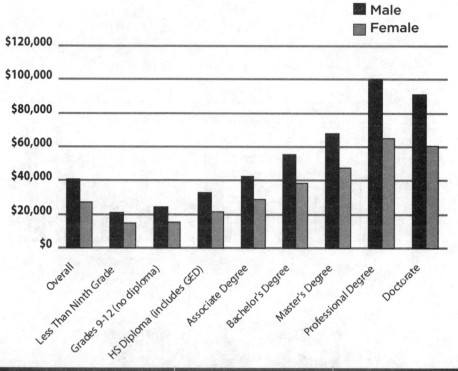

Educational attainment	Number of persons (in thousands) with income		Median income, in 2006 dollars	
	Male	Female	Male	Female
Overall	71,657	62,412	$40,837	$27,337
Less Than Ninth Grade	3,207	1,596	$21,079	$14,455
Grades 9–12 (no diploma)	5,311	3,219	$24,092	$15,162
HS Diploma (includes GED)	21,810	17,751	$33,074	$21,609
Associate Degree	5,990	7,071	$42,462	$29,091
Bachelor's Degree	14,989	14,100	$55,425	$38,221
Master's Degree	5,439	5,547	$67,992	$47,586
Professional Degree	1,658	900	$100,000	$65,107
Doctorate	1,405	672	$91,051	$60,448

Source: U.S. Census Bureau, *2007 Current Population Survey,*
2007 Annual Social and Economic Supplement

NOTE: The U.S. Census Bureau publishes income and poverty data each year for the previous calendar year.
For the most current information provided in this format, visit www.ahaprocess.com.

U.S. Per-Capita, Median Household, and Median Family Income, in 2006 Dollars: 1967 to 2006

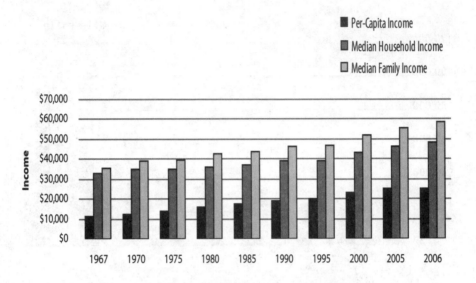

Year	Per-Capita Income	Median Household Income	Median Family Income
2006	$25,267	$48,451	$58,526
2005	25,035	46,242	55,832
2000	22,970	43,162	52,148
1995	19,871	39,306	46,843
1990	18,894	39,324	46,429
1985	17,280	37,059	43,518
1980	15,844	36,035	42,776
1975	13,972	34,980	39,784
1970	12,543	35,232	39,954
1967	11,067	32,783	35,629

Source: U.S Census Bureau,
2007 American Community Survey

NOTE: The U.S. Census Bureau publishes income and poverty data each year for the previous calendar year. For the most current information provided in this format, visit www.ahaprocess.com.

Percentage of U.S. Persons Below Poverty Level, by Race and Ethnicity: 1976 to 2006

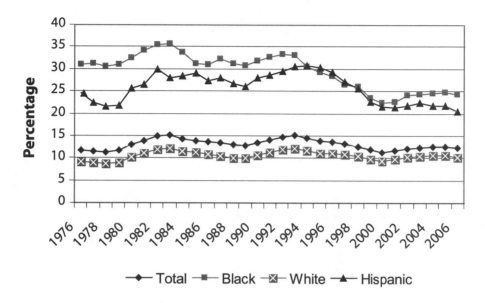

Year	Total	Black	White	Hispanic
2006	12.3	24.3	10.3	20.6
2005	12.6	24.9	10.6	21.8
2004	12.7	24.7	10.8	21.9
2003	12.5	24.4	10.5	22.5
2002	12.1	24.1	10.2	21.8
2001	11.7	22.7	9.9	21.4
2000	11.3	22.5	9.5	21.5
1999	11.9	23.6	9.8	22.7
1998	12.7	26.1	10.5	25.6
1997	13.3	26.5	11.0	27.1
1996	13.7	28.4	11.2	29.4
1995	13.8	29.3	11.2	30.3
1994	14.5	30.6	11.7	30.7
1993	15.1	33.1	12.2	30.6
1992	14.8	33.4	11.9	29.6
1991	14.2	32.7	11.3	28.7

Year	Total	Black	White	Hispanic
1990	13.5	31.9	10.7	28.1
1989	12.8	30.7	10.0	26.2
1988	13.0	31.3	10.1	26.7
1987	13.4	32.4	10.4	28.0
1986	13.6	31.1	11.0	27.3
1985	14.0	31.3	11.4	29.0
1984	14.4	33.8	11.5	28.4
1983	15.2	35.7	12.1	28.0
1982	15.0	35.6	12.0	29.9
1981	14.0	34.2	11.1	26.5
1980	13.0	32.5	10.2	25.7
1979	11.7	31.0	9.0	21.8
1978	11.4	30.6	8.7	21.6
1977	11.6	31.3	8.9	22.4
1976	11.8	31.1	9.1	24.7

Source: U.S. Census Bureau;
data for 2006 released in 2007

NOTE: The U.S. Census Bureau publishes income and poverty data each year for the previous calendar year. For the most current information provided in this format, visit www.ahaprocess.com.

Research Notes

AUTHOR'S NOTE: The following Research Notes have been selected to correlate with the content of this book. The quotations and sourcing are intended to supplement, not replace, the Bibliography. The intent also is to buttress the primary premises of this book with the perspectives of many other keen observers in the field. It is the author's hope that this book and these notes will spark further study of—and caring involvement in—the culture of survival in North America.

Introduction

How do we break the cycle? Educate the parents, especially the mothers, of the children in school; "the educational level of mothers is the most important influence on the educational attainment of children."

Lewis, Anne C. "Breaking the Cycle of Poverty." *Phi Delta Kappan.* November 1996. Volume 78. Number 3. p. 186.

"Mayer reviewed studies and tried to match parents' incomes with children's outcomes. Good outcomes were high test scores, having a job (or being in school) at the age of 24 and earning high wages. Bad outcomes included dropping out of high school and becoming an unwed mother. Of course, children of middle class parents do better than children of poorer parents."

Samuelson, Robert J. "The Culture of Poverty." *Newsweek.* May 5, 1997. Volume 129. Number 18. p. 49.

Banfield described the situationally poor: The group lacking money—comprising the disabled, the unemployed, and some single mothers. They had middle-class values, "could benefit from government income support," and "could usually recover from a setback (job loss, divorce)."

Ibid.

The extended family:

When a break is made from the extended family, the person may feel he has more control of his own life, yet he's "threatened by the loss of a sense of fraternity with people you value."

Sennett, Richard, and Cobb, Jonathan. *The Hidden Injuries of Class.* London/Boston: Faber and Faber, 1993. First published in U.S.A. in 1972 by Alfred A. Knopf, New York, NY. p. 110.

By the early 20th century, it was recognized that "many children were destitute because their fathers had died or deserted them."

Mayer, Susan E. *What Money Can't Buy.* Cambridge, MA: Harvard University Press, 1997. p. 21.

Child poverty rates in the U.S. are high when they are compared with other rich industrial countries' rates: in the mid-1980s (most recent data available):
- 1.6%—Sweden
- 2.8%—Germany
- 4.6%—France
- 7.4%—United Kingdom
- 9.3%—Canada
- 20.4%—U.S.A.

(from House Ways and Means Committee 1993, p. 1453)

Ibid. p. 39.

Better outcomes for children result with each additional year of parental education.

Ibid. p. 153.

From 1987 to 1996, in any given year of that time period, 12 to 14 million children (or about one in five) lived in poverty.

Brooks-Gunn, Jeanne, Duncan, Greg J., and Maritato, Nancy. Poor Families, Poor Outcomes: The Well-being of Children and Youth. Duncan, Greg J., and Brooks-Gunn, Jeanne, Editors. *Consequences of Growing Up Poor.* New York, NY: Russell Sage Foundation, 1997. p. 1.

One important cause of the increase in child poverty rates is the increase in numbers of single parents—due either to divorce or children being born outside of marriage.
   1990: Two-thirds of black women and 19% of white women had children outside of marriage (Ventura, 1995).

Ibid. p. 4.

"Poverty rates are high for children in families with one adult, particularly because employment rates are high for children in families with one adult, particularly because employment rates are low among single mothers, many of whom are young and have not completed high school."

Ibid.

"Poverty rates for children in families in which a divorce has occurred are high, especially since incomes for custodial mothers drop precipitously after a divorce" (McLanahan and Sandefur, 1994; Duncan, 1991, Chapter 3)."

Ibid.

The number of single mothers has also risen because the divorce rate is higher than the remarriage rate.

Ibid.

There is a greater likelihood of black and Hispanic children being poor than white children. They are also more likely to be poor for a longer time period.

Ibid. p. 5.

"Mothers' education is a strong and consistent predictor of children's outcomes—from IQ test scores at age five through school completion rates at age nineteen and twenty" (Duncan, Brooks-Gunn, and Klebanov, 1994; Haveman and Wolfe, 1995). "It is unclear whether the effects of mothers' education are larger or smaller than those of family income."

Ibid. p. 13.

"While the rise of mother-only families is without doubt increasingly important as a proximate cause of childhood poverty, the historical analysis presented here strongly suggests that employment insecurity and low earnings for fathers continue to be prime determinants of the levels of and the trends in childhood poverty, both because of their direct effect on family income and because of their indirect contribution to the rise in mother-only families. This analysis also strongly suggests that mothers' employment has become increasingly important in determining childhood poverty levels and trends, both directly because of the income mothers bring into the home and indirectly by facilitating separation and divorce."

Hernandez, Donald J. Poverty Trends. Duncan, Greg J., and Brooks-Gunn, Jeanne, Editors. *Consequences of Growing Up Poor.* New York, NY: Russell Sage Foundation, 1997. p. 33.

"About half of mother-only families in the U.S. are poor during any given year." ... "About 50% of mother-only families receive welfare during the course of a year, and a nontrivial proportion are on welfare for long periods of time."

McLanahan, Sara E. Parent Absence or Poverty: Which Matters More? Duncan, Greg J., and Brooks-Gunn, Jeanne, Editors. *Consequences of Growing Up Poor.* New York, NY: Russell Sage Foundation, 1997. p. 35.

"Poverty rates are two to three times higher for children whose mothers have never married or have divorced."

Smith, Judith R., Brooks-Gunn, Jeanne, and Klebanov, Pamela K. Consequences of Living in Poverty for Young Children's Cognitive and Verbal Ability and Early School Achievement. Duncan, Greg J., and Brooks-Gunn, Jeanne, Editors. *Consequences of Growing Up Poor.* New York, NY: Russell Sage Foundation, 1997. p. 135.

"Children who spend more time in poverty are less likely to graduate from high school, obtain fewer years of schooling, and earn less."

Teachman, Jay D., Paasch, Kathleen M., Day, Randal D., and Carver, Karen P. Poverty During Adolescence and Subsequent Educational Attainment. Duncan, Greg J., and Brooks-Gunn, Jeanne, Editors. *Consequences of Growing Up Poor.* New York, NY: Russell Sage Foundation, 1997. p. 383.

"Children who had spent one to three years of their adolescence in a family below the poverty line were about 60% less likely to graduate from high school than children who had never been poor. Children who had spent four years of their adolescence living in a family below the poverty line were about 75% less likely to graduate from high school ... On average, children who had spent some or all of their adolescence living in poverty obtained between 1.0 and 1.75 fewer years of schooling than other children."

Ibid. p. 388.

"Parents' education (particularly the mother's education) had a positive relationship with each educational outcome." (Outcomes in this study were: high school graduation, college enrollment, and years of schooling completed.)

Ibid. p. 398.

"Our findings indicate that poverty was negatively related to high school graduation, college attendance, and years of schooling obtained. However, much of the observed relationship can be attributed to differences in a number of control variables, such as parental education, family structure, and IQ. After the control variables were taken into account, the number of years spent below the poverty line during adolescence were not related to any of the educational outcomes considered."

Ibid. p. 413.

"Poor parents have less schooling, on average, than do nonpoor parents, and schooling may affect parents' abilities to encourage and help their children to get an education."

Corcoran, Mary, and Adams, Terry. Race, Sex, and the Intergenerational Transmission of Poverty. Duncan, Greg J., and Brooks-Gunn, Jeanne, Editors. *Consequences of Growing Up Poor.* New York, NY: Russell Sage Foundation, 1997. p. 463.

"The breakup of a marriage (or the parents' failure to marry) increases the chance that a child will be poor during childhood, may lead to psychological distress, may reduce parental supervision, and may limit the child's role models for marriage and work. The distress, lack of supervision, and lack of role models could in turn lead children to be poor as adults."

Ibid.

"For example, poor families are also more likely to be headed by a single parent, a parent with low educational attainment, an unemployed parent, a parent in the low-wage market, a divorced parent, or a young parent. These familial conditions might account in large measure for the association between low income and less favorable outcomes for children."

Brooks-Gunn, Jeanne, Duncan, Greg J., and Maritato, Nancy. Poor Families, Poor Outcomes: The Well-being of Children and Youth. Duncan, Greg J., and Brooks-Gunn, Jeanne, Editors. *Consequences of Growing Up Poor.* New York, NY: Russell Sage Foundation, 1997. p. 1.

"The demographic trends in family patterns and in individual behavior—changes in marriage and divorce rates, nonmarital fertility rates, and unemployment rates (especially for less educated and younger adults) —help explain the relative increase in the proportion of children in poverty."

Ibid. p. 4.

"By 1993, 22.7% of children were officially classified as poor, the highest poverty rate experienced by children since the mid-1960s."

Hernandez, Donald J. Poverty Trends. Duncan, Greg J., and Brooks-Gunn, Jeanne, Editors. *Consequences of Growing Up Poor*. New York, NY: Russell Sage Foundation, 1997. p. 18.

In 1993, 23% of children lived with their mother and with no father in the home; from 1940 to 1960, this percentage was 6 to 8% and 20% in 1990—due to divorce rates increasing and out-of-wedlock births increasing.

Ibid. p. 30.

In 1995, 40% of children lived apart from one parent. It's estimated that more than 50% of the children born in the early 1980s will be in the same situation prior to reaching 18 years of age (Bumpass, 1984).

McLanahan, Sara S. Parent Absence or Poverty: Which Matters More? Duncan, Greg J., and Brooks-Gunn, Jeanne, Editors. *Consequences of Growing Up Poor*. New York, NY: Russell Sage Foundation, 1997. p. 35.

". . . [C]hildren who grow up with only one biological parent are less successful, on average, than children who grow up with both parents. These differences extend to a broad range of outcomes and they persist into adulthood" (McLanahan and Sandefur, 1994; Haveman and Wolfe, 1991; Cherlin and Furstenberg, 1991; Amato and Keith, 1991; Seltzer, 1994).

Ibid. p. 37.

The National Center for Children in Poverty (NCCP), based at Columbia University, has tracked child poverty rates (under 6 years old) from 1975 to 1994. The NCCP study reports that "the young child poverty rate has grown to include one in four young children and that nearly 50 percent of American young children are near poverty or below."

Wake Up America: Columbia University Study Shatters Stereotypes of Young Child Poverty. Internet Web site: *http://cpmcnet.columbia.edu/news*/press_releases/12-11-96.html. December 11, 1996.

"In 1994, a shocking 45 percent of young children—nearly half—were in poverty or near poverty (with incomes below 185 percent of the federal poverty line)."

Ibid.

"Between 1975 and 1994, the young child poverty rate increased by 39 percent, leaving one in four young children (25 percent) in poverty, and the rate of young children in extreme poverty (with incomes below 50 percent of the poverty line) doubled, from 6 to 12 percent." | Ibid.

"[T]he young child poverty rate grew twice as fast for whites (38 percent) as for blacks (19 percent)." | Ibid.

"[Y]oung children living in traditional nuclear families, with two parents where one parent is employed full-time, were 2½ times as likely to be poor. Their poverty rate grew from 6 to 15 percent." | Ibid.

"In addition, most poor children live in working families, contrary to the commonly-held belief that a family job will keep children out of poverty. In 1994, 62 percent of poor young children lived with at least one parent or relative who worked part time or full time." | Ibid.

"[T]he young child poverty rate grew nearly twice as fast in the suburbs (59 percent) as in urban areas (34 percent)." | Ibid.

Youth in America are the poorest among us, and their numbers continue to increase. | "The Poorest Among Us." *U.S. News & World Report.* December 23, 1996. Volume 121. Number 25. p. 18.

6.1 million children under age 6 lived in poverty in 1994. This number almost equals the combined population of Chicago and Los Angeles. The number means one in four of these children are in poverty. | Ibid.

"While minority youngsters are far more likely to be poor than whites, more than a third of all poor kids are white. And they have joined the ranks of the poor at twice the rate that blacks have." | Ibid.

"Child poverty is spreading fastest in the suburbs. Still, urban kids are most likely to be poor—40% in some cities." | Ibid.

"More children in two-parent families fell into poverty—mainly as a result of lower-paying jobs. And 62% of poor kids now have a parent who works at least part time." | Ibid.

Jack Levine, who is with the Florida Center for Children and Youth, said, " 'None of us is immune to the concerns of children who aren't ready for education, whose health needs are served in emergency rooms and who do not have the family support to keep them out of trouble.' "

Ibid.

In the 1964 State of the Union address, the war on poverty was declared. The President's Council of Economic Advisors reported there was "an inverse relationship between the extent of education of family heads and the incidence of poverty."

Seligman, Ben B. The Numbers of Poor. Penchef, Esther, Editor. *Four Horsemen: Pollution, Poverty, Famine, Violence.* San Francisco, CA: Canfield Press, 1971. p. 93.

Causes of poverty include poor education, obsolete skills, ill health, divorce, desertion, alcohol, and drugs.

Dicks, Lee E. The Poor Who Live Among Us. Penchef, Esther, Editor. *Four Horsemen: Pollution, Poverty, Famine, Violence.* San Francisco, CA: Canfield Press, 1971. p. 118.

"Death, divorce, desertion, and illegitimacy deprive many families of a male breadwinner, and this unquestionably contributes to poverty."

Ibid. p. 120.

"The Navajos on their reservation in Arizona are a good example of poverty surrounded by opulence, and of the 'invisible poor.' Their circumstances demonstrate how the definition of poverty is relative to the situation."

U.S. News & World Report. Where the Real Poverty Is: Plight of American Indians. Penchef, Esther, Editor. *Four Horsemen: Pollution, Poverty, Famine, Violence.* San Francisco, CA: Canfield Press, 1971. p. 155.

"The rise of the single-parent family has led to increased poverty among both adults and children."

Harrington, Michael. *The Other America.* New York, NY: Simon & Schuster, 1962. p. xv.

"Perhaps the most important factor in the increase of poverty during the 1980s has been the steady decline in wage levels, so that we now have in America a group we call the working poor—people who do have jobs, who work hard, who try desperately to stay afloat as providers [for] families (sometimes men, sometimes

Ibid. pp. xv–xvi.

women) but who earn such wretchedly low wages that they sink below the poverty line."

Some of the evidence to support the changes in family life includes:

> "One of every two marriages in the United States currently ends in divorce . . . Each year, more than 1.5 million children—nearly 2.5 percent of all U.S. children—undergo the painful experience of seeing their parents separate or divorce."

Zill, Nicholaus. "The Changing Realities of Family Life." *Aspen Institute Quarterly.* Winter 1993. Volume 5. Number 1. pp. 29–30.

> "Marriage rates have declined, and a growing proportion of adults are forgoing or at least deferring legal marriage."

Ibid.

> "The number of children born outside of marriage is growing."

Ibid.

> "Large numbers of adult females are raising children on their own, often in poverty or welfare dependency. In 1991, there were 11.7 million female-headed families in the United States, and 36 percent of them, 4.2 million, were poor. Female-headed families made up more than half of all poor families in the country in contrast to 1959, when fewer than 2 million female-headed families lived in poverty, and constituted only 23 percent of all poor families" (data from U.S. Bureau of the Census, *Poverty in the United States: 1991.* Current Population Reports, Series F-60, Number 181. Washington, DC: GPO, August 1992).

Ibid.

"Among other things, family factors have implications for childhood poverty, welfare dependency, injury, illness, premature death, adolescent childbearing, developmental and mental health disorders in children, delinquency and violent behavior in young adults, alcoholism and substance abuse. Cause and effect relationships underlying these associations have not always been clearly established, but there is certainly enough evidence to warrant public policy focus on family factors."

Ibid. p. 32.

"In the last several years, public unease about the state of American children has burgeoned along with anxieties about the family, and for closely related reasons. However, the 'children's problem' is really several different problems, involving different processes and distinct

Ibid. p. 35.

portions of the youth population. The first and probably most serious of these dilemmas is that of childhood poverty, or 'children at risk.' The concern here is that a substantial minority of today's young people are being raised in disadvantaged circumstances that seriously impede their chances of growing into healthy, responsible, productive members of adult society."

In the section on *Recent Trends in Poverty*, Zill writes, "Childhood poverty is also more common in families lacking full-time, year-round workers; in families in which parents have low achievement test scores and education levels; in young families; and in minority families. Studies indicate that the increase in child poverty is due to *both* the growth of single-parent families and the deteriorating earning power of young parents, especially those with limited educations."

Ibid. p. 37.

"Economic conditions have changed such that, in order to ensure a decent standard of living and avoid poverty, a child needs to have both parents working. Yet, because of increases in divorce and unmarried child-bearing, and a decline in the propensity of single mothers to marry or remarry, fewer young children are living with both parents in married-couple families. Moreover, payment of child support is typically minimal and irregular. Indeed, fewer poor children have even one parent working. Hence, today's young children in poverty are more likely to be persistently poor. In addition, more poor children, especially those in central cities, are living in high-poverty neighborhoods where the risks to their development are particularly severe."

Ibid.

"But few doubt that children in low-income families are in developmental jeopardy because of the conditions that often accompany or foster poverty, such as low parent education levels, family, disorganization, limited opportunities, rundown housing, bad schools and hazardous neighborhood conditions."

Ibid. p. 38.

"*The U.S. economy has changed in ways that make it hard for young families to 'play by the rules' and do well.* Technological developments, the globalization of the U.S. economy and changes in the distribution of income and assets have made it harder for young families, especially those in which the parents have only a high school education or less, to work and earn enough to support themselves and their children. The growth of child poverty has not been due simply to the increase in female-headed households—even that trend is partly attributable to the changing earning prospects of young males, especially African-American and Hispanic males."

Ibid. p. 48.

The author makes several points "that contradict the preconceived notions of many liberal child advocates." One of these is: *"Many problems of today's children do stem from detrimental behavior patterns, either those of parents or of young people themselves.* Liberals should acknowledge the truth of the conservative contention that many problems of today's children and families have their roots in detrimental behavior patterns, rather than in a lack of opportunity or a lack of resources."

Ibid. p. 49.

Chapter One: Definitions and Resources

Without literacy skills, a child will probably be unable to break out of the "intergenerational cycles of poverty."

Lewis, Anne C. "Breaking the Cycle of Poverty." *Phi Delta Kappan.* November 1996. Volume 78. Number 3. p. 186.

In Susan Mayer's book, *What Money Can't Buy*, she asks the question: "[H]ow important is money in enabling families to help their children escape poverty?" It doesn't matter much.

Samuelson, Robert J. "The Culture of Poverty." *Newsweek.* May 5, 1997. Volume 129. Number 18. p. 49.

In another study, Mayer and Christopher Jencks of Harvard note that poor children's "material well being" improved, but this didn't result in improved social conditions.

Ibid.

A character in a scenario views poverty "as depriving men of the capacity to act rationally, to exercise self-control"—educated people are thought to be able to do this.

Sennett, Richard, and Cobb, Jonathan. *The Hidden Injuries of Class.* London/Boston: Faber and Faber, 1993. First published in U.S.A. in 1972 by Alfred A. Knopf, New York, NY. p. 22.

Knowledge gained through formal education provides "the tools for achieving freedom—by permitting [men] to control situations and by furnishing [them] with access to a greater set of roles in life."	Ibid. p. 30.
The extended family:	Ibid. pp. 106–107.
Provides the basis for interdependent relationships with regard to (1) calling upon relatives in times of financial or marital difficulties; (2) child-rearing duties; and (3) economic discussions, such as buying a house.	
"[I]s a defense that has sheltered both black and white poor in cities."	
While helpful, it can also be binding—"others are always in one's personal affairs."	
"The 'parental-stress' theory holds that poverty is stressful and that stress diminishes parents' ability to provide appropriate and effective parenting. The 'role model' theory holds that because of their position at the bottom of the social hierarchy, low-income parents develop values, norms, and behaviors that cause them to be 'bad' role models for their children."	Mayer, Susan E. *What Money Can't Buy.* Cambridge, MA: Harvard University Press, 1997. p. 7.
One controversial version of the role-model hypothesis contends that income transfers won't change "values and behavior" of "those enmeshed in a 'culture of poverty.'"	Ibid. pp. 7–8.
Child poverty rate in 1990 was 19.9% (U.S. Bureau of the Census, 1993, tables 736 and 739).	Ibid. p. 39.
Money buys goods, services, and experiences.	Ibid. p. 98.
"Parental income is not as important to children's outcomes as some social scientists have thought. This is because the parental characteristics that employers value and are willing to pay for, such as skills, diligence, honesty, good health, and reliability, also improve children's life chances, independent of their effect on parents' income."	Ibid. pp. 2–3.
When a family experiences "short-term poverty," it is rare that family members change their values.	Ibid. p. 52.

Income affects children's well-being. Income allows parents to provide safer home environments; better schools, parks, libraries; higher education; good health care; and other things that benefit the health and development of the children.

Brooks-Gunn, Jeanne, Duncan, Greg J., and Maritato, Nancy. Poor Families, Poor Outcomes: The Well-being of Children and Youth. Duncan, Greg J., and Brooks-Gunn, Jeanne, Editors. *Consequences of Growing Up Poor.* New York, NY: Russell Sage Foundation, 1997. p. 14.

"A promising line of research has begun to link poverty to the emotional well-being of children" (McLeod and Shanahan, 1993). "Elder et al. (1992) have shown that economic loss is associated with shifts in parenting practices, with negative consequences for the emotional well-being of children. Family stress and the lack of learning resources that are associated with poverty probably dampen the likelihood of high school completion."

Haveman, Robert, Wolfe, Barbara, and Wilson, Kathryn. Childhood Poverty and Adolescent Schooling and Fertility Outcomes: Reduced-form and Structural Estimates. Duncan, Greg J., and Brooks-Gunn, Jeanne, Editors. *Consequences of Growing Up Poor.* New York, NY: Russell Sage Foundation, 1997. p. 415.

"Specifically, characteristics of neighborhoods and schools are likely to influence the educational progress of children" (Snow et al., 1991; Wilson, 1987). "The choices families make concerning neighborhoods and schools affect the social environment within which children interact outside the home. These patterns of social interaction are likely to structure the opportunities and constraints perceived by adolescents as they make decisions about the relevance of continued education" (Crane, 1991; Mayer, 1991c; Mayer & Jencks, 1989).

Ibid.

"According to Becker (1981), families allocate resources between current consumption and investments in children's human capital. Poor parents will need most of their resources for economic survival and will have little time, money, and energy left over to invest in children's human capital."

Corcoran, Mary, and Adams, Terry. Race, Sex, and the Intergenerational Transmission of Poverty. Duncan, Greg J., and Brooks-Gunn, Jeanne, Editors. *Consequences of Growing Up Poor.* New York, NY: Russell Sage Foundation, 1997. p. 462.

"Poor parents may be less able to afford housing in 'good' neighborhoods (i.e., safe neighborhoods with high-quality schools and good role models) and may be less connected to job networks than all nonpoor parents" (Loury, 1981; Coleman, 1990).

Ibid.

"Loury (1981), Massey (1991), and Wilson (1987, 1991a, 1991b, 1993) contend that access to 'good' neighborhoods (and hence the ability to increase children's social capital) is even more restricted for poor, minority parents because of 'tastes,' historical housing discrimination, and current housing discrimination."

Ibid.

"The breakup of a marriage (or the parents' failure to marry) increases the chance that a child will be poor during childhood, may lead to psychological distress, may reduce parental supervision, and may limit the child's role models for marriage and work. The distress, lack of supervision, and lack of role models could in turn lead children to be poor as adults."

Ibid. p. 463.

In a study by Wilson, he "emphasizes that working parents and employed neighbors provide children with role models for work and that middle-class neighbors are important both as socializing agents and as sources of 'social control.'"

Ibid. p. 464.

"Low income and other economic hardships may reduce children's self-esteem by reducing the emotional or supportive qualities of the parents' home. The pressure that limited economic resources can place on marital relationships can, in turn, translate into negative parent-child relations and lower levels of self-esteem."

Axinn, William, Duncan, Greg J., and Thornton, Arland. The Effects of Parents' Income, Wealth, and Attitudes on Children's Completed Schooling and Self-Esteem. Duncan, Greg J., and Brooks-Gunn, Jeanne, Editors. *Consequences of Growing Up Poor.* New York, NY: Russell Sage Foundation, 1997. p. 521.

Boyd is used as an example of a person without a car; he and his wife have to get a taxi or find a neighbor to take them to the hospital where they receive free care when their sons experience severe asthma attacks. They could have a phone at home because the fits are bad enough (welfare would allow it) but they can't afford one.

Dicks, Lee E. The Poor Who Live Among Us. Penchef, Esther, Editor. *Four Horsemen: Pollution, Poverty, Famine, Violence.* San Francisco, CA: Canfield Press, 1971. p. 122.

The author says that middle-class persons "find it relatively easy to locate the appropriate agency for help and redress" when dealing with frustrations stemming from public bureaucracy. "On the other hand, the typical ghetto resident has interrelated social and economic problems which require the services of several government and private agencies. At the same time, he may be unable to identify his problems in terms of the complicated structure of government. Moreover, he may be unaware of his rights and opportunities under public programs and unable to obtain the necessary guidance from either public or private sources."

Ritchie, Barbara. What Can Be Done. Penchef, Esther, Editor. *Four Horsemen: Pollution, Poverty, Famine, Violence.* San Francisco, CA: Canfield Press, 1971. p. 169.

The author describes the difficulties she encounters in trying to transfer her checking account to another branch of the bank from where she'd originally opened it. She was originally able to open it because a friend (her publisher) took her to her bank to meet with a bank representative. Because of the publisher's knowledge of her, she was allowed to open an account. She had no credit card, no driver's license; this time she was able to make the transfer only because she knew the bank president.

Capponi, Pat. *Dispatches from the Poverty Line.* Toronto, Ontario, Canada: Penguin Books, 1997. pp. 82–85.

One person the author interviews who tells her story says, " 'I feel so bad for those without the emotional supports I have, without family and friends.' "

Ibid. p. 134.

In describing her friends she chose when she was 13, Lisa said, " 'They were kids who lived in housing projects like Regent Park, Donmount Court. Kids who spent late nights in clubs, dancing and drinking and smoking dope. I was the only one who had to lie about what I was doing—either their mothers were just too tired from working all day to try and enforce rules, or they were nurses doing night shifts. There didn't seem to be any fathers living at home.' "

Ibid. pp. 175–176.

Lisa quit school in Grade 10 and got a job. She said, " 'Of course, the only work I could get were low-paying, service-oriented jobs that did nothing to make me feel better about who I was.' "

Ibid. p. 176.

"But their humor and easy ways were contained in an environment of misery. I remember families who could not send their children to school because there were not enough shoes for all. One family passed the shoes from child to child, so that at least a couple of them would be in school each day."

Harrington, Michael. *The Other America.* New York, NY: Simon & Schuster, 1962. p. 99.

An example of two girls who were promiscuous in New Haven was given: "When the girl from Class I [the rich] was arrested, she was provided with bail at once, newspaper stories were quashed, and she was taken care of through private psychotherapy. The girl from Class V [the poor] was sentenced to reform school. She was paroled in two years, but was soon arrested again and sent to the state reformatory."

Ibid. p. 128.

"In the slum, conduct that would shock a middle-class neighborhood and lead to treatment is often considered normal. Even if someone is constantly and violently drunk, or beats his wife brutally, people will say of such a person, 'Well, he's a little odd.' Higher up on the class scale an individual with such a problem would probably realize that something was wrong (or his family would). He will have the knowledge and the money to get help."

Ibid. p. 129.

"And finally, the family of the poor lives cheek and jowl with other families of the poor. The sounds of all the quarreling and fights of every other family are always present if there happens to be a moment of peace in one household. The radio and the television choices of the rest of the block are regularly in evidence. Life is lived in common, but not in community."

Ibid. p. 136.

"In short, being poor is not one aspect of a person's life in this country; it is his life. Taken as a whole, poverty is a culture. Taken on the family level, it has the same quality. These are the people who lack education and skill, who have bad health, poor housing, low levels of aspiration and high levels of mental distress."

Ibid. p. 162.

"A series of drastic alterations in patterns of family living in the United States has occurred in the last 30 years."

Zill, Nicholaus. "The Changing Realities of Family Life." *Aspen Institute Quarterly.* Winter 1993. Volume 5. Number 1. p. 29.

"Low income children interviewed by the National Commission on Children, particularly those living in urban environments, were far more likely to fear for their own safety and less likely to enjoy social supports or to feel that neighborhood resources were accessible and safe than children from more affluent families."

Ibid. p. 38.

In a study that "made use of data from two national surveys of families with children," it was found "that only about one-third of children in low-income families received stimulation and support from their parents comparable to that received by most children in families that were neither poor nor welfare dependent."

Ibid. pp. 38–39.

" 'I pray. I talk to God. I tell Him, "Lord, it is your work. Put me to rest at night and wake me in the morning." ' "

Kozol, Jonathan. *Amazing Grace.* New York, NY: Crown Publishers, 1995. p. 169.

"Children who have had the benefits of preschool and one of the better elementary schools are at a great advantage in achieving entrance to selective high schools; but an even more important factor seems to be the social class and education level of their parents. This is the case because the system rests on the initiative of parents. The poorest parents, often the products of inferior education, lack the information access and the skills of navigation in an often hostile and intimidating situation to channel their children to the better schools, obtain the applications, and (perhaps a little more important) help them to get ready for the necessary tests and then persuade their elementary schools to recommend them. So, even in poor black neighborhoods, it tends to be children of the less poor and the better educated who are likely to break through the obstacles and win admission."

Kozol, Jonathan. *Savage Inequalities.* New York, NY: Harper Perennial, 1991. p. 60.

Chapter Two: The Role of Language and Story

"At the core of the problems of those on or nearly on welfare is the inadequacy of the schools' efforts to teach what they should first and foremost—language." Children must learn to read, write, speak, and listen.

Lewis, Anne C. "Breaking the Cycle of Poverty." *Phi Delta Kappan.* November 1996. Volume 78. Number 3. pp. 186–187.

How do we break the cycle? Start literacy enrichment in the delivery room; cognition research and infant development studies show "that early language stimulation—from the moment of birth—influences brain development and later learning success." There should be "support networks" to help young parents from poor means in developing their child's language abilities.

Ibid. p. 187.

"My mother in her broken English could remedy few of the injustices, but she tried."

Rodriguez, Luis J. *Always Running*. New York, NY: Simon & Schuster, 1993. p. 21.

"In school, they placed Rano in classes with retarded children because he didn't speak much English."

Ibid.

The author says when he went to school he was put in the back of the classroom to play with blocks because he couldn't speak English.

Ibid. p. 26.

He didn't want to be misunderstood, so he seldom asked questions.

Ibid. p. 27.

"The fact was I didn't know anything about literature. I had fallen through the chasm between two languages. The Spanish had been beaten out of me in the early years of school—and I didn't learn English very well either. "This was the predicament of many Chicanos. "We could almost be called incommunicable, except we remained lucid; we got over what we felt, sensed and understood. Sometimes we rearranged words, created new meanings and structures—even a new vocabulary. Often our everyday talk blazed with poetry. "Our expressive powers were strong and vibrant. If this could be nurtured, if the language skills could be developed on top of this, we could learn to break through any communication barrier. We needed to obtain victories in language, built on an infrastructure of self-worth. "But we were often defeated from the start."

Ibid. p. 219.

"One girl wrote in an essay that she experiences rejection and ridicule from schoolmates when she speaks what she considers 'proper' English. They accuse her of 'acting white' and of trying to deny her African heritage, charges that upset her greatly."

Fox, Steven. "The Controversy over Ebonics." *Phi Delta Kappan.* November 1997. Volume 79. Number 3. p. 239.

Psychologists know that basic language patterns are formed very early, with the basic language structures firmly in place by age 5. We learn language, perhaps the most complex of all of our systems of knowledge, by imitation rather than by prescription. That is, we make sentences and follow the patterns of language long before we can explicitly state the rules of grammar or syntax, if we are ever able to do so. Childhood errors are replaced, usually without instruction, with standard forms because the child hears the language used by adults. Children in environments where SAE is the language spoken will develop the patterns of that dialect themselves and will do so very early in their lives."

Ibid. p. 240.

Chapter Three: Hidden Rules Among Classes

Mayer says America has " 'vacillated between trying to improve the material well-being of poor children and . . . the moral character of their parents' " for 200 years.

Samuelson, Robert J. "The Culture of Poverty." *Newsweek.* May 5, 1997. Volume 129. Number 18. p. 49.

The test of "welfare reform" is fewer teen pregnancies, more marriages that are stable and children living in "better homes," not a reduction in welfare cases.

Ibid.

"Mayer writes: 'The parental characteristics that employers value and are willing to pay for, such as skills, diligence, honesty, good health, and reliability, also improve children's life chances, independent of their effect on parents' incomes. Children of parents with these attributes do well even if their parents do not have much income.' "

Ibid.

Reference to "middle class *things*."

Sennett Richard, and Cobb Jonathan. *The Hidden Injuries of Class.* London/ Boston: Faber and Faber, 1993. First published in U.S.A. in 1972 by Alfred A. Knopf, New York, NY. p. 18.

A character in a story/scenario knows the "rules of middle-class life."

Ibid. p. 21.

Children at the Watson School did not feel that the time in the classroom was " 'real time.' " Instead "they would come alive" when they were able to go to work and be "on their own." Adults on the job view their time at work the same way. In an example, one individual felt that " 'the job's just cash to live; the things that matter every day to me are at home . . . the family, people . . . the neighborhood.' "

Ibid. p. 93.

Goal for most individuals: "[M]aterial things are aids to creating an inner self which is complex, variegated, not easily fathomed by others—because only with such psychological armor can a person hope to establish some freedom within the terms of a class society."	Ibid. p. 258.
Theories of why poor children fail more often than rich children: (1) "Parents who are present-oriented, fatalistic, and unambitious raise children who are the same. Both generations tend to be jobless and poor." (2) Material deprivation and parental stress of poverty cause failure because children can't compete if their basic needs are not met.	Mayer, Susan E. *What Money Can't Buy.* Cambridge, MA: Harvard University Press, 1997. p. 16.
The definitions of class by each group: People at the bottom define class by your amount of money; people in middle class value education and your line of work almost as much as money; at the top, people emphasize "taste, values, ideas, style, and behavior"—regardless of money, education, or occupation.	Fussel, Paul. *Class.* New York, NY: Ballantine Books, 1983. p. 3.
Middle class is characterized by " 'Correctness' and doing the right thing."	Ibid. p. 34.
A sign of middle class: desire to belong and to do so by a "mechanical act," such as purchasing something.	Ibid. p. 35.
Middle class: believes in the "likelihood of self-improvement."	Ibid. p. 37.
Upper middle class: The emphasis of cookbooks, and books about food and food presentation addressed to them, was about " 'elegance.' " At their dinner parties, the guests are an audience.	Ibid. p. 111.
"At the very top, the food is usually not very good, tending, like the conversation, to a terrible blandness, a sad lack of originality and cutting edge."	Ibid. p. 113.
Middle class is the main clientele for mail-order catalogs; "the things they buy from them assure them of their value and support their aspirations."	Ibid. p. 132.
Buying things, especially from mail-order catalogs, is a way "the middle and [proletarian] classes assert their value."	Ibid. p. 131.

"If it's grammar that draws the line between middles and below, it's largely pronunciation and vocabulary that draw it between middle and upper."	Ibid. p. 178.
The farther down socially one moves, the more likely that the TV set will be on.	Ibid. p. 100.
A sign of the upper classes is silence; proles are identified by noise and vociferation.	Ibid. p. 196.
A Chicago policeman, probably a high prole, said, "'If my mother and father argued, my mother went around shutting down the windows because they didn't want the neighbors to hear 'em. But they [i.e., the lower sort of proles] deliberately open the doors and open the windows, screaming and hollering . . .' "	Ibid.
Proles like to be called "'Mr. [First Name] Prole.'"	Ibid. p. 197.
Low-income families differ from higher-income families in more ways than just economics (i.e., they're not as likely to have the two biological parents living in the household, to have adults with college degrees or high-status jobs present); "they are more likely to live in poor neighborhoods, receive income from welfare, contain adults with mental or physical problems, and so on."	Brooks-Gunn, Jeanne, Duncan, Greg J., and Maritato, Nancy. Poor Families, Poor Outcomes: The Well-being of Children and Youth. Duncan, Greg J., and Brooks-Gunn, Jeanne, Editors. *Consequences of Growing Up Poor.* New York, NY: Russell Sage Foundation, 1997. p. 14.
"In communities with limited resources like Humboldt Park and East L.A., sophisticated survival structures evolved, including gangs, out of the bone and sinew tossed up by this environment."	Rodriguez, Luis J. *Always Running.* New York, NY: Simon & Schuster, 1993. p. 8.
The author says that in the first Christmas his family had (the presents were from a church group), "I broke the plastic submarine, toy gun and metal car I received. I don't know why. I suppose in my mind it didn't seem right to have things in working order, unspent."	Ibid. pp. 22–23.
When the family moved from South Central L.A. to Reseda after their dad obtained a substitute teaching job, he writes, "Even my brother enjoyed success in this new environment. He became the best fighter in the school . . ."	Ibid. pp. 30–31.

Rodriguez says his dad "went nuts in Reseda," buying things such as new furniture, a new TV, a new car. He went into debt to do so, but "his attitude was 'who cares.' We were Americans now." But then his dad lost his job, and these things were repossessed.

Ibid. p. 31.

"It seemed Mama was just there to pick up the pieces when my father's house of cards fell."

Ibid.

During the time in Reseda, his mother was "uncomfortable." . . . "The other mothers around here were good-looking, fit and well-built. My pudgy mom looked dark, Indian and foreign, no matter what money could buy."

Ibid.

"It seems to me that the culture of poverty has some universal characteristics which transcend regional, rural-urban, and even national differences. In my earlier book, *Five Families* (Basic Books, 1959), I suggested that there were remarkable similarities in family structure, interpersonal relations, time orientations, value systems, spending patterns, and the sense of community in lower-class settlements in London, Glasgow, Paris, Harlem, and Mexico City. Although this is not the place for an extensive comparative analysis of the culture of poverty, I should like to elaborate upon some of these and other traits in order to present a provisional conceptual model of this culture based mainly upon my Mexican materials."

Lewis, Oscar. The Culture of Poverty. Penchef, Esther, Editor. *Four Horsemen: Pollution, Poverty, Famine, Violence.* San Francisco, CA: Canfield Press, 1971. p. 137.

"The economic traits which are most characteristic of the culture of poverty include the constant struggle for survival, unemployment and underemployment, low wages, a miscellany of unskilled occupations, child labor, the absence of savings, a chronic shortage of cash, the absence of food reserves in the home, the pattern of frequent buying of small quantities of food many times a day as the need arises, the pawning of personal goods, borrowing from local money lenders at usurious rates of interest, spontaneous informal credit devices *(tandas)* organized by neighbors, and the use of second-hand clothing and furniture."

Ibid. pp. 137–138.

"... [T]he city jail is one of the basic institutions of the other America."	Harrington, Michael. The Invisible Land. Penchef, Esther, Editor. *Four Horsemen: Pollution, Poverty, Famine, Violence.* San Francisco, CA: Canfield Press, 1971. p. 153.
In a conversation the author describes "work hard, get ahead" as a "middle class promise."	Capponi, Pat. *Dispatches from the Poverty Line.* Toronto, Ontario, Canada: Penguin Books, 1997. p. 41.
The author says she "didn't spend a lot of time worrying about nutrition, just volume enough to quell hunger pains."	Ibid. p. 53.
"The poor are usually as confined by their poverty as if they lived in a maximum security prison. There is not much exposure to other ways of life, unless their neighborhood starts to undergo gentrification."	Ibid. pp. 82–85.
In describing her friend Nora's situation, the author writes: "Born into what I think of as the 'lost-out' generation, just pre-baby boom, Nora says there wasn't much questioning going on: you obeyed your parents and your teachers; middle-class values and expectations weren't suspect, everyone you knew bought into them. You provided your children with at least as much as you had, and that meant, for a divorced woman, getting a job. Nora's mother still works, at eighty-eight, bound and determined not to be a burden to her children. It's what a responsible person does, Nora believed."	Ibid. p. 161.
The author, when writing about going to Nora's for a dinner party, says: "I can ask them about the invisible rules that become visible only when you break them. If they say, 'Come about seven,' I can demand clarification: what does that really mean? I don't settle for, 'Whenever you get here,' I hold out for what's socially acceptable."	Ibid. p. 166.
Lisa, an interviewee, says: " 'I never felt like I was middle class. I didn't live in a renovated house, we didn't have cable or colour television, junk food, ketchup in bottles, new cars, yearly family vacations.'	Ibid. pp. 173–174.

My mother says: 'Of course you were raised in a middle-class family. You went to camp, you took gymnastics and ballet, you read books for entertainment, both your parents were educated and working.' "

Lisa continues: " 'But to me, it seemed that second-hand clothes and home cooking (we never went to restaurants) were less of a lifestyle choice than an economic necessity. This is not to say I felt I was poor. I got everything I needed, just not what I wanted. I was envious of my friends. While we only had two channels on a black-and-white TV, a huge treat was going to lunch at my girlfriend's. We'd eat hot dogs and watch 'The Flintstones.' It seemed at the time they had all the luxuries: Pop Tarts for breakfast, white bread, while at home I was crunching stale granola and wheat germ and watching my mother make ketchup out of tomatoes and molasses.' "

Ibid.

"But the new poverty is constructed so as to destroy aspiration; it is a system designed to be impervious to hope."

Harrington, Michael. *The Other America.* New York, NY: Simon & Schuster, 1962. p. 10.

"This is how the Midtown researchers described the 'low social economic status individual': they are 'rigid, suspicious and have a fatalistic outlook on life. They do not plan ahead, a characteristic associated with their fatalism. They are prone to depression, have feelings of futility, lack of belongingness, friendliness, and a lack of trust in others.' "

Ibid. p. 133.

Of the poor, the author says that, "they do not postpone satisfactions that they do not save. When pleasure is available, they tend to take it immediately."

Ibid. p. 134.

"Like the Asian peasant, the impoverished American tends to see life as a fate, an endless cycle from which there is no deliverance."

Ibid. p. 161.

Class I: "the rich, usually aristocrats of family as well as of money." Class V: "the bottom class, was made up of the poor."

Ibid. p. 123.

The elite are said to "accept one another, understand one another, marry one another, tend to work and to think if not together at least alike."

Mills, C. Wright. *The Power Elite.* New York, NY: Oxford University Press, 1956. p. 11.

"No matter what else they may be, the people of these higher circles are involved in a set of overlapping 'crowds' and intricately connected 'cliques.'"

Ibid.

". . . [T]here is the increased seasonal change of residence among both rural and small-town upper classes. The women and children of the rural upper class go to 'the lake' for the summer period, and the men for long weekends, even as New York families do the same in the winters in Florida."

Ibid. p. 40.

The upper social class "belong to clubs and organizations to which others like themselves are admitted, and they take quite seriously their appearances in these associations."

Ibid. p. 57.

"They have attended the same or similar private and exclusive schools, preferably one of the Episcopal boarding schools of New England. Their men have been to Harvard, Yale, Princeton, or if local pride could not be overcome, to a locally esteemed college to which their families have contributed."

Ibid. p. 58.

"The one deep experience that distinguishes the social rich from the merely rich and those below is their schooling, and with it, all the associations, the sense and sensibility, to which this education routine leads throughout their lives."

Ibid. p. 63.

"As a selection and training place of the upper classes, both old and new, the private school is a unifying influence, a force for the nationalization of the upper classes."

Ibid. p. 64.

"The major economic fact about the very rich is the fact of the accumulation of advantages: those who have great wealth are in a dozen strategic positions to make it yield further wealth."

Ibid. p. 115.

In describing the rich: ". . . [T]heir toys are bigger; they have more of them; they have more of them all at once."

Ibid. p. 164.

Reverend Gregory Groover says many of the children in the South Bronx don't go to Manhattan. He says, "'. . . Some have never traveled as far as 125th Street, which is close to us, in Harlem.'" He tells about a boy they call Danny. "'. . . He was 16 before he ever went across the bridge into New Jersey when I took him with me on a trip I had to make. He told me, "I thought New Jersey was this state out there near California." . . .'"

Kozol, Jonathan. *Amazing Grace*. New York, NY: Crown Publishers, 1995. p. 81.

Chapter Four: Characteristics of Generational Poverty

The extended family "makes the dependence of family members on each other into a code of honor." This works by age usually, "the older people having a right to set the standard for the younger."	Sennett, Richard, and Cobb, Jonathan. *The Hidden Injuries of Class.* London/Boston: Faber and Faber, 1993. First published in U.S.A. in 1972 by Alfred A. Knopf, New York, NY. p. 106.
In describing a factory worker, his wife speaks of his ability related to sports statistics, and he says, " 'She shouldn't make anything of it; I mean, I didn't.' " . . . "There is something more here than embarrassment at being praised. The strengths 'I' have are not admissible to the arena of ability where they are socially useful; for once admitted, 'I'—my real self—would no longer have them."	Ibid. p. 216.
Low-income parents compared to rich parents: Are not as likely to be married. Typically have less education. Typically have poorer health.	Mayer, Susan E. *What Money Can't Buy.* Cambridge, MA: Harvard University Press, 1997. p. 8.
The role-model version of the good-parent theory contends that "because of their position at the bottom of the social hierarchy, low-income parents develop values, norms, and behaviors that are 'dysfunctional' for success in the dominant culture."	Ibid. p. 50.
Men and women from low-income background are less likely to marry when they have a child than those from higher income. When they marry, "they are more likely to separate and divorce."	Ibid. pp. 65–66.
"Absent any state support, some women and children will be more likely to remain in abusive and destructive relationships with men. Others will turn to 'social prostitution,' serial relationships with men willing to pay their bills."	Ibid. pp. 151–152.

"Poor parents differ from rich parents in many ways besides income. For instance, low-income parents usually have less education and are less likely to marry, which could also explain disparities in rich and poor children's life chances."

Mayer, Susan E. Trends in the Economic Well-being and Life Chances of America's Children. Duncan, Greg J., and Brooks-Gunn, Jeanne, Editors. *Consequences of Growing Up Poor.* New York, NY: Russell Sage Foundation, 1997. p. 51.

"Clearly, poverty experienced during adolescence negatively affects the educational attainment of children. The role played by education in determining the economic and occupational success of Americans suggests longer-term consequences. The consequences of dropping out of high school are particularly drastic: over the past two decades, individuals with less than a high school degree have suffered an absolute decline in real income and have dropped further behind individuals with more education."

Teachman, Jay D., Paasch, Kathleen M., Day, Randal D., and Carver, Karen P. Poverty During Adolescence and Subsequent Educational Attainment. Duncan, Greg J., and Brooks-Gunn, Jeanne, Editors. *Consequences of Growing Up Poor.* New York, NY: Russell Sage Foundation, 1997. p. 416.

"Our estimates of the determinants of the teen out-of-wedlock birth outcome suggest that parental characteristics (the education of the mother) are important determinants of teens' childbearing choices but that poverty itself is not a significant determinant. However, having income well above the poverty line does appear to reduce teen out-of-wedlock births. A family characteristic frequently associated with poverty— the number of years spent living with a single parent —is also a significant determinant of teenage fertility choices, particularly if a child spends the teenage years from twelve to fifteen living in poverty."

Haveman, Robert, Wolfe, Barbara, and Wilson, Kathryn. Childhood Poverty and Adolescent Schooling and Fertility Outcomes: Reduced-form and Structural Estimates. Duncan, Greg J., and Brooks-Gunn, Jeanne, Editors. *Consequences of Growing Up Poor.* New York, NY: Russell Sage Foundation, 1997. p. 443.

"The number of unmarried women having children has risen dramatically, and childbirth outside of marriage is not confined to teenagers."

Brooks-Gunn, Jeanne, Duncan, Greg J., and Maritato, Nancy. Poor Families, Poor Outcomes: The Well-being of Children and Youth. Duncan, Greg J., and Brooks-Gunn, Jeanne, Editors. *Consequences of Growing Up Poor.* New York, NY: Russell Sage Foundation, 1997. p. 4.

"Criminality in this country is a class issue. Many of those warehoused in overcrowded prisons can be properly called 'criminals of want,' those who've been deprived of the basic necessities of life and therefore forced into so-called criminal acts to survive . . . They are members of a social stratum which includes welfare mothers, housing project residents, immigrant families, the homeless and unemployed."

Rodriguez, Luis J. *Always Running.* New York, NY: Simon & Schuster, 1993. p. 10.

He says his mother "held up the family when almost everything else came apart."

Ibid. p. 23.

"We changed houses often because of evictions."

Ibid. p. 30.

The family then moved in with Seni, the author's half-sister, and her family. A grandmother also lived there, making a total of 11 in the apartment. "The adults occupied the only two bedrooms. The children slept on makeshift bedding in the living room." The author and his brother "sought refuge in the street."

Ibid. p. 32.

"We didn't call ourselves gangs. We called ourselves clubs or *clicas* . . . It was something to belong to— something that was ours. We weren't in [B]oy [S]couts, in sports teams or camping groups. Thee Imperson-ations (club name) is how we wove something out of threads of nothing."

Ibid. p. 41.

"But 'family' is a farce among the propertyless and disenfranchised. Too many families are wrenched apart, as even children are forced to supplement meager incomes. Family can only really exist among those who can afford one."

Ibid. p. 250.

"Even when income is used to define poverty, one finds relatively high ownership of televisions and automobiles among the poor."

Seligman, Ben B. The Numbers of Poor. Penchef, Esther, Editor. *Four Horsemen: Pollution, Poverty, Famine, Violence.* San Francisco, CA: Can-field Press, 1971. p. 95.

"Poverty does different things to different people. Walk into the home of a poor family. A stench may offend the nostrils; filth may offend the eyes. Or the home may look immaculate."

Dicks, Lee E. The Poor Who Live Among Us. Penchef, Esther, Editor. *Four Horsemen: Pollution, Poverty, Famine, Violence.* San Francisco, CA: Canfield Press, 1971. p. 118.

An example of Rosita's neighbor is given: She has five children by five different men—she's never had a husband.

Ibid. p. 120.

Boyd and his wife believe education provides the best chance for his son. He said, " '. . . [T]hey won't get any place at all without high school education, and most likely college to boot.' "

Ibid. p. 123.

"Some of the social and psychological characteristics include living in crowded quarters, a lack of privacy, gregariousness, a high incidence of alcoholism, frequent resort to violence in the settlement of quarrels, frequent use of physical violence in the training of children, wife beating, early initiation into sex, free unions or consensual marriages, a relatively high incidence of the abandonment of mothers and children, a trend toward mother-centered families and a much greater knowledge of maternal relatives, the predominance of the nuclear family, a strong predisposition to authoritarianism, and a great emphasis upon family solidarity—an ideal only rarely achieved. Other traits include a strong present time orientation with relatively little ability to defer gratification and plan for the future, a sense of resignation and fatalism based upon the realities of their difficult life situation, a belief in male superiority which reaches its crystallization in *machismo* or the cult of masculinity, a corresponding martyr complex among women, and finally, a high tolerance for psychological pathology of all sorts."

Lewis, Oscar. The Culture of Poverty. Penchef, Esther, Editor. *Four Horsemen: Pollution, Poverty, Famine, Violence.* San Francisco, CA: Canfield Press, 1971. p. 138.

Family structure of the poor: "more homes without a father, there is less marriage, more early pregnancy and, if Kinsey's statistical finding can be used, markedly different attitudes toward sex. As a result of this, to take but one consequence of the fact, hundreds of thousands, and perhaps millions, of children in the other America never know stability and 'normal' affection."

Harrington, Michael. The Invisible Land. Penchef, Esther, Editor. *Four Horsemen: Pollution, Poverty, Famine, Violence.* San Francisco, CA: Canfield Press, 1971. p. 153.

"First rule of the streets: don't display weakness, sentimentality."	Capponi, Pat. *Dispatches from the Poverty Line.* Toronto, Ontario, Canada: Penguin Books, 1997. p. 150.
The author asks an interviewer how she feels about hooking. The response is: " 'You just turn off part of your mind. You gotta think, well, a guy goes out, he buys work boots, and he puts them to work to make money. I put my body to work. It's the same thing, really.' "	Ibid. p. 153.
The author describes the poor in America as being "pessimistic and defeated."	Harrington, Michael. *The Other America.* New York, NY: Simon & Schuster, 1962. p. 2.
"Poverty in the United States is a culture, an institution, a way of life."	Ibid. p. 16.
"He (F. Scott Fitzgerald) understood that being rich was not a single fact, like a large bank account, but a way of looking at reality, a series of attitudes, a special type of life. If this is true of the rich, it is ten times truer of the poor. Everything about them, from the condition of their teeth to the way in which they love, is suffused and permeated by the fact of their poverty."	Ibid.
"There is, in short, a language of the poor, a psychology of the poor, a world view of the poor. To be impoverished is to be an internal alien, to grow up in a culture that is radically different from the one that dominates society."	Ibid. p. 17.
In describing men who worked in coal mines but who were laid off, Swados says, " 'It is truly ironic that a substantial portion of these men, who pride themselves on their ability to live with danger, to work hard, to fight hard, drink hard, love hard, are now learning housework and taking over the woman's role in the family.' "	Ibid. p. 28.
"As often happens in the culture of poverty, marriage was somewhat irregular among these folk. The women were not promiscuous—they lived with one man at a time, and for considerable periods. But, after some years and a child or two, the marriage would break up. It was not uncommon to meet two or three sets of half-brothers and half-sisters living under the same roof."	Ibid. p. 98.

"And yet this grim description, like the account of a Negro ghetto, misses the quality of life. As one walked along the streets in the late summer, the air was filled with hillbilly music from a hundred radios. There was a sort of loose, defeated gaiety about the place, the casualness of a people who expected little. These were poor Southern whites."

Ibid. p. 99.

"But within a slum, violence and disturbance are often norms, everyday facts of life. From the inside of the other America, joining a 'bopping' gang may well not seem like deviant behavior. It could be a necessity for dealing with a hostile world. (Once, in a slum school in St. Louis, a teacher stopped a fight between two little girls. 'Nice girls don't fight,' she told them. 'Yeah,' one of them replied, 'you should have seen my old lady at the tavern last night.'")

Ibid. p. 127.

"Related to this pattern of immediate gratification is a tendency on the part of the poor to 'act out,' to be less inhibited, and sometimes violent."

Ibid. p. 135.

"In New Haven, for instance, Hollingshead and Redlich found that in Class V (the poor) some 41% of the children under seventeen lived in homes that had been disrupted by death, desertion, separation, or divorce."

Ibid.

Regarding family structures among the poor, Yale researchers found that "23% grew up in a 'generation stem family,' where different generations are thrown together, usually with a broken marriage or two. Under such circumstances there is the possibility of endless domestic conflict [among] the different generations (and this is exacerbated when the old are immigrants with a foreign code). Another 18% came from broken homes where one or the other parent was absent. And 11% had experienced the death of a parent."

Ibid. pp. 135–136.

"Another aspect of this family pattern is sexual. In New Haven the researchers found that it was fairly common for young girls in the slums to be pregnant before they were married. I saw a similar pattern in St. Louis. There, children had a sort of sophisticated ignorance about sexual matters at an early age. Jammed together in miserable housing, they knew the facts of sex from firsthand observation (though often what they saw was a brutalized and drunken form of sex)."

Ibid. p. 136.

"Perhaps the most important analytic point to have emerged in this description of the other America is the fact that poverty in America forms a culture, a way of life and feeling, that it makes a whole. It is crucial to generalize this idea, for it profoundly affects how one moves to destroy property."

Ibid. pp. 159–160.

"On another level, the emotions of the other America are even more profoundly disturbed. Here it is not lack of aspiration and of hope; it is a matter of personal chaos. The drunkenness, the unstable marriages, the violence of the other America are not simply facts about individuals. They are the description of an entire group in the society who react this way because of the conditions under which they live."

Ibid. p. 162.

Some of the evidence to support the changes in family life includes: "Large numbers of adult males are only loosely attached to the families and households that contain their offspring. Many among these see their children sporadically, if at all, and contribute little or nothing to the financial support of their children."

Zill, Nicholaus. "The Changing Realities of Family Life." *Aspen Institute Quarterly.* Winter 1993. Volume 5. Number 1. p. 37.

When walking with five children (two are 7 years old, two are 9 years old, and the other is described as a tiny child), Kozol says: "None of the children can tell me the approximate time that school begins. One says five o'clock. One says six. Another says that school begins at noon." The children then tell him of the rape and murder of one of their sisters.

Kozol, Jonathan. *Savage Inequalities.* New York, NY: Harper Perennial, 1991. pp. 12–13.

A 12-year-old boy named Jeremiah tells Kozol that " 'white people started moving away from black and Spanish people in New York' " in 1960. Kozol asks him where the white people went. Another boy says he thinks they moved to the country. Jeremiah then says, " 'It isn't where people live. It's *how* they live.' " Kozol asks him to repeat what he said. " 'It's *how* they live,' he says again. 'There are different economies in different places.' " Kozol asks Jeremiah to explain what he means, and Jeremiah refers to Riverdale, "a mostly white and middle-class community in the northwest section of the Bronx." " 'Life in Riverdale is opened up,' he says. 'Where we live, it's locked down.' " Kozol asks him, " 'In what way?' " He responds, " 'We can't go out and play.' "

Kozol, Jonathan. *Amazing Grace.* New York, NY: Crown Publishers, 1995. p. 32.

A 15-year-old student, Isabel, says she thinks Jeremiah's description of feeling " 'locked down' " is "too strong." " 'It's not like being in a jail,' she says. 'It's more like being "hidden." It's as if you have been put in a garage where, if they don't have room for something but aren't sure if they should throw it out, they put it where they don't need to think of it again.' "

Ibid. pp. 38–39.

Chapter Five: Role Models and Emotional Resources

"But in a study of the New York State Commission Against Discrimination an even more serious situation was described: one in which Negro children had more aspiration than whites from the same income level, but less opportunity to fulfill their ambition . . . The Negro child, coming from a family in which the father has a miserable job, is forced to reject the life of his parents, and to put forth new goals for himself. In the case of the immigrant young some generations ago, this experience of breaking with the Old Country tradition and identifying with the great society of America was a decisive moment in moving upward. But the Negro does not find society as open as the immigrant did."

Harrington, Michael. *The Other America*. New York, NY: Simon & Schuster, 1962. pp. 77–78.

Chapter Six: Support Systems

Chronic low income results in "coping strategies and material deprivations that are detrimental to children's behavior."

Mayer, Susan E. *What Money Can't Buy*. Cambridge, MA: Harvard University Press, 1997. p. 76.

"Other fruitful strategies might be more indirect programmatic ones, such as helping mothers read more to their children (as well as read more themselves) and teaching mothers about intellectually stimulating learning activities that they can do at home with their children" (Brooks-Gunn, Denner, and Klebanov, 1995; Snow, 1986).

Smith, Judith R., Brooks-Gunn, Jeanne, and Klebanov, Pamela K. Consequences of Living in Poverty for Young Children's Cognitive and Verbal Ability and Early School Achievement. Duncan, Greg J., and Brooks-Gunn, Jeanne, Editors. *Consequences of Growing Up Poor*. New York, NY: Russell Sage Foundation, 1997. p. 167.

"Parents' economic resources can influence self-esteem in several ways. Parents' income brings both parents and children social status and respect that can translate into individual self-esteem. Income can also enhance children's self-esteem by providing them with the goods and services that satisfy individual aspirations."

Axinn, William, Duncan, Greg J., and Thornton, Arland. The Effects of Parents' Income, Wealth, and Attitudes on Children's Completed Schooling and Self-esteem. Duncan, Greg J., and Brooks-Gunn, Jeanne, Editors. *Consequences of Growing Up Poor.* New York, NY: Russell Sage Foundation, 1997. p. 521.

In models by Rand D. Conger, Kathy J. Conger, and Glen Elder, "[L]ow income produces economic pressures that can lead to conflict between parents over financial matters, which in turn affects the harshness of the mother's parenting and the adolescent's self-confidence and achievement."

Duncan, Greg J., and Brooks-Gunn, Jeanne. Income Effects Across the Life Span: Integration and Interpretation. Duncan, Greg J., and Brooks-Gunn, Jeanne, Editors. *Consequences of Growing Up Poor.* New York, NY: Russell Sage Foundation, 1997. p. 602.

The author makes several points that he says "conservatives may find troublesome." One of these includes: "*Federal programs have made a difference in children's lives.* As noted earlier, the character of child poverty in this country has been changed for the better by programs such as food stamps, WIC, Medicaid, Chapter 1 and equal opportunity efforts."

Zill, Nicholaus. "The Changing Realities of Family Life." *Aspen Institute Quarterly.* Winter 1993. Volume 5. Number 1. pp. 47–48.

Chapter Seven: Discipline

"If generations of irregular employment and discrimination result in street skills seeming more valuable than academic skills, parents will be more likely to encourage their children to acquire street skills than to study or stay in school."

Mayer, Susan E. *What Money Can't Buy.* Cambridge, MA: Harvard University Press, 1997. p. 51.

A school counselor said, " 'Giving the family money can improve the standard of living, but it won't give the children the tools they will need for success.' Her

Ibid. p. 113.

colleague added, 'I think it is the parenting values—the parenting style—that matters more than the money.' "

"'Power-assertive' disciplinary techniques"—physical punishment, valuing obedience, and not being supportive of their children—are used by poor parents more so than other parents.

Ibid. p. 115.

"Because poverty is associated with symptoms of stress, and because symptoms of stress are associated with poor parenting practices, many researchers infer that poverty leads to bad parenting practices, which then cause worse outcomes among children."

Ibid.

He said his father "didn't get angry or hit me. That he left to my mother."

Rodriguez, Luis J. *Always Running*. New York, NY: Simon & Schuster, 1993. p. 47.

An example of punishment was given. He said his mother "carved into my flesh with a leather belt."

Ibid. p. 74.

"Across domains, family structure appears to be more important in some areas of children's well-being than in others. *Behavioral problems* show the most consistent negative effects. All four of the studies that examined children's outcomes in this domain found that a parent's absence was associated with more behavioral problems. Hanson, McLanahan, and Thomson (chapter 8) found that family disruption increased school behavior problems. Pagani, Boulerice, and Tremblay (chapter 11) found more fighting and hyperactivity among children from nonintact families, and Lipman and Offord found evidence of social impairment. In addition, Haveman, Wolfe, and Wilson (chapter 14) found that girls from nonintact families were more likely to become unwed teen mothers than were girls from intact families."

McLanahan, Sara S. Parent Absence or Poverty: Which Matters More? Duncan, Greg J., and Brooks-Gunn, Jeanne, Editors. *Consequences of Growing Up Poor*. New York, NY: Russell Sage Foundation, 1997. p. 40.

Chapter Eight: Instruction and Improving Achievement

"The higher the income of a family, the more education succeeding generations receive."

Lewis, Anne C. "Breaking the Cycle of Poverty." *Phi Delta Kappan*. November 1996. Volume 78. Number 3. p. 186.

"Children raised in low-income families score lower than children from more affluent families do on assessments of health, cognitive development, school achievement, and emotional well-being."

Brooks-Gunn, Jeanne, Duncan, Greg J., and Maritato, Nancy. Poor Families, Poor Outcomes: The Well-being of Children and Youth. Duncan, Greg J., and Brooks-Gunn, Jeanne, Editors. *Consequences of Growing Up Poor.* New York, NY: Russell Sage Foundation, 1997. p. 1.

"Evidence from this study shows that family poverty affected the cognitive abilities of children in two very different samples, as measured at separate ages . . . Effects of income were found at each age from two to eight years."

Smith, Judith R., Brooks-Gunn, Jeanne, and Klebanov, Pamela K. Consequences of Living in Poverty for Young Children's Cognitive and Verbal Ability and Early School Achievement. Duncan, Greg J., and Brooks-Gunn, Jeanne, Editors. *Consequences of Growing Up Poor.* New York, NY: Russell Sage Foundation, 1997. p. 164.

"Children who lived in persistently poor families scored 6-9 points lower on the various assessments than children who were never poor."

Ibid.

"Indeed, parents' education is always linked to young children's outcomes."

Ibid. p. 166.

In the researchers' analyses, "[T]he home experience mediated the effects of the mother's education more strongly than family income. This finding fits with the belief that education is linked to specific ways of talking, playing, interacting, and reading with young children" (Bradley et al., 1989; Sugarland et al., 1995). "It also suggests that working on increasing the educational levels of mothers will affect children via their home experiences, a tenet upon which many early childhood intervention programs are based" (Chase-Lansdale and Brooks-Gunn, 1995; Clarke-Stewart and Fein, 1983).

Ibid. pp. 166–167.

"In sum, income and tax benefits aimed at increasing the family income of poor families, as well as early intervention programs aimed at improving the home learning environment, for parents and children, would improve the school readiness and cognitive ability of the nations' youngest citizens."

Ibid. p. 167.

"From a reanalysis of Glueck and Glueck's (1950) retrospective data on the prediction of juvenile delinquency, Sampson and Laub (1994) conclude that 'poverty appears to inhibit the capacity of families to achieve informal social control, which in turn increases the likelihood of adolescent delinquency.'"

Pagani, Linda, Boulerice, Bernard, and Tremblay, Richard E. The Influence of Poverty on Children's Classroom Placement and Behavior Problems. Duncan, Greg J., and Brooks-Gunn, Jeanne, Editors. *Consequences of Growing Up Poor.* New York, NY: Russell Sage Foundation, 1997. p. 311.

"The duration of poverty mattered for cognitive development, but timing did not influence children's outcomes" (from Duncan, Brooks-Gunn, and Klebanov, 1994; data analyses from the Infant Health and Development Program).

Ibid. p. 334.

". . . [T]he number of years adolescents lived in poor families was an important predictor of school attainment and early career achievements" (from Corcoran et al., 1992).

Ibid.

"Some evidence suggests that duration of poverty may influence mediating factors. Garrett, Ng'andu, and Ferron (1994) observed that the longer children reside in poverty, the lower the quality of their family environment. However, a competing argument maintains that parents' social adjustment and cognitive competence prior to parenthood could explain the relationship between the persistence of poverty and cognitive outcomes" (Benson et al., 1993; Serbin et al., 1991).

Ibid.

"A child's family income appears to significantly affect changes in cognitive performance between ages 3 and 12 but not changes in internalizing and externalizing behaviors."

Ibid. p. 337.

"The amount of parental time available while growing up (including the presence of two parents in the home) and having fewer siblings is positively related to educational attainment. Both the educational level of the mother and the economic resources available to the family (proxied by both total family income and the number of years that the family is in poverty) are related to educational success. In particular, the number of years in poverty appears to be an important determinant of the probability of graduating [from] high school. Other things being equal, children who grow up in poor families are far less likely than other children to complete high school. When these children also grow up with only a single parent, the probability that they will complete high school is further reduced."

Haveman, Robert, Wolfe, Barbara, and Wilson, Kathryn. Childhood Poverty and Adolescent Schooling and Fertility Outcomes: Reduced-form and Structural Estimates. Duncan, Greg J., and Brooks-Gunn, Jeanne, Editors. *Consequences of Growing Up Poor.* New York, NY: Russell Sage Foundation, 1997. pp. 441–442.

"The research literature is also beginning to suggest that the emotional and supportive quality of the parental home rather than its structure or composition most strongly influences a child's sense of self-worth" (Demo and Acock, 1988; Raschke, 1987).

Axinn, William, Duncan, Greg J., and Thornton, Arland. The Effects of Parents' Income, Wealth, and Attitudes on Children's Completed Schooling and Self-esteem. Duncan, Greg J., and Brooks-Gunn, Jeanne, Editors. *Consequences of Growing Up Poor.* New York, NY: Russell Sage Foundation, 1997. p. 521.

"Whitbeck et al. (1991) found that family economic hardship, as reported by parents, affected self-esteem indirectly 'by decreasing parental support and involvement' (1991). They found, however, that reported economic hardship had only weak direct effects on children's self-esteem, which appears consistent with the work of other researchers, who have found parental behavior toward children to be an important determinant of children's self-esteem" (Gecas and Schwalbe, 1986; Demo, Small, and Savin-Williams, 1987).

Ibid.

"Family income has large effects on some measures of the children's ability and achievement, but not on the behavior, mental health, or physical health measures represented by the developmental studies in chapters 5, 7, 11, 14, 16, and 17."

Duncan, Greg J., and Brooks-Gunn, Jeanne. Income Effects Across the Life Span: Integration and Interpretation. Duncan, Greg J., and Brooks-Gunn, Jeanne, Editors.

Consequences of Growing Up Poor. New York, NY: Russell Sage Foundation, 1997. p. 597.

"Family economic conditions in early and middle childhood appear to be far more important for shaping ability and achievement than they do during adolescence."

Ibid.

"Family income is usually a stronger predictor of ability and achievement outcomes than are measures of parental schooling or family structure."

Ibid.

". . . [T]he quality of the home environment—its opportunities for learning, the warmth of mother-child interactions, and the physical condition of the home— accounts for a substantial portion of the powerful effects of family income on cognitive outcomes."

Ibid. p. 601.

Family structure has effect on: test scores, grade-point average, and years of school—modest effects. Behavioral-problem indicators like skipping school and early childbearing—more substantial effects.

McLanahan, Sara S. Parent Absence or Poverty: Which Matters More? Duncan, Greg J., and Brooks-Gunn, Jeanne, Editors. *Consequences of Growing Up Poor.* New York, NY: Russell Sage Foundation, 1997. p. 37.

Income accounts for "about 50% of the difference in educational attainment of children raised in one- and two-parent families." The remaining differences for one-parent children are attributed to receiving less "parental supervision" (especially from fathers) and having less "social capital" because they move more frequently.

Ibid.

All of the research teams except one, Teachman et al., found that "a parent's absence had negative consequences for children's school achievement." The teams: (1) Hanson, McLanahan, and Thomson; (2) Conger, Conger, and Elder; (3) Lipman and Offord; (4) Pagani, Boulerice, and Tremblay (negative effects on school performance); (5) Peters and Mullis; (6) Haveman, Wolfe, and Wilson (less likely to graduate from high school if from nonintact family; (7) Peters and Mullis; and (8) Hauser and Sweeney (lower rates of college attendance and graduation).

Ibid. p. 41.

"The fact that family disruption has stronger and more consistent effects on educational attainment than on test scores suggests that something besides cognitive ability is responsible for the poorer school performance of children from nonintact families." | Ibid.

"These findings suggest the net effects of poverty on cognitive ability and school achievement are equal to or larger than the net effects of family disruption." | Ibid. p. 47.

Regarding educational attainment, children in step-families do better than those in single-parent families, but they do worse in the areas of behavioral and psychological problems. | Ibid.

"In practical terms, because children living in persistent poverty appear to be at greater risk for serious academic failure, their potential contribution to society remains limited." | Pagani, Linda, Boulerice, Bernard, and Tremblay, Richard E. The Influence of Poverty on Children's Classroom Placement and Behavior Problems. Duncan, Greg J., and Brooks-Gunn, Jeanne, Editors. *Consequences of Growing Up Poor.* New York, NY: Russell Sage Foundation, 1997. p. 338.

"A variety of factors have been found to be consistently related to the schooling attainments of children; the parents' education, the family's income, the number of parents in the child's family, the parents' expectations, and characteristics of the child's school and teachers are among the more important" (Haveman and Wolfe, 1995). | Haveman, Robert, Wolfe, Barbara, and Wilson, Kathryn. Childhood Poverty and Adolescent Schooling and Fertility Outcomes: Reduced-form and Structural Estimates. Duncan, Greg J., and Brooks-Gunn, Jeanne, Editors. *Consequences of Growing Up Poor.* New York, NY: Russell Sage Foundation, 1997. p. 421.

"However, the importance of money in enabling parents to purchase better learning environments for their children is reinforced by the National Institute for Child Health and Human Development Child Care | Duncan, Greg J., and Brooks-Gunn, Jeanne. Income Effects Across the Life Span: Integration and

Research Network's data on early child care (Chapter 6), which showed that family income was a significant determinant of the quality of nearly all of the child care environments observed, including center-based child care."

Interpretation. Duncan, Greg J., and Brooks-Gunn, Jeanne, Editors. *Consequences of Growing Up Poor*. New York, NY: Russell Sage Foundation, 1997. p. 602.

Children's scores on cognitive assessments are affected by the number of books a child has and the frequency of visits to a museum.

Mayer, Susan E. *What Money Can't Buy*. Cambridge, MA: Harvard University Press, 1997. p. 10.

"Low income decreases the quality of nonmonetary investments, such as parents' interactions with their children."

Ibid. p. 48.

Chapter Nine: Creating Relationships

When talking about his brother and a teacher he had, the author says, "Mrs. Snelling saw talent in Rano, a spark of actor during the school's thespian activities. She even had him play the lead in a class play. He also showed some facility with music. And he was good in sports . . . So when I was at Garvey, he was in high school being the good kid, the Mexican exception, the barrio success story—my supposed model. Soon he stopped being Rano or even Jose. One day he became Joe."

Rodriguez, Luis J. *Always Running*. New York, NY: Simon & Schuster, 1993. p. 49.

The author writes: "I spent a lot of time in a lot of groups trying to get people to see each other as people. To relate to one another not as social worker to patient, not as psychiatrist to patient, but as people. Most of all, to learn to value what is good and decent about people, whatever their circumstances. It's sad that that's something we have to learn from and about people whose chief struggle, of all the struggles they have to fight, is for the right to contribute and to be seen as contributing members of the society that once rejected them."

Capponi, Pat. *Dispatches from the Poverty Line*. Toronto, Ontario, Canada: Penguin Books, 1997. pp. 187–188.

"It seems to me sometimes that we take a person in poverty, an individual suffering the misery of poverty, and we subdivide that misery into sections. Then we build huge support systems based on our assumptions about those stand-alone bits of misery:

Ibid.

welfare
children's aid
corrections
addictions
shelters
food banks
psychiatry
drop-ins

"And while we successfully continue to employ all the helpers in the helping professions, and sometimes make great strides in treating one particular bit of misery, we continue to fail to see the individual and the source from which all the misery springs."	Ibid.
"The operation is a success, but the patient dies."	Ibid.

Conclusion

Her study also challenges the thought that "if pushed, the poor can become self-sufficient through work." It, in essence, supports "the existence of a permanent 'culture of poverty,' an argument first advanced in the modern American context by political scientist Edward Banfield in a 1970 book."	Samuelson, Robert J. "The Culture of Poverty." *Newsweek.* May 5, 1997. Volume 129. Number 18. p. 49.
Freedom is now defined by the amount of choice a person has and by "the development of human resources of men and women in a post scarcity society."	Sennett, Richard, and Cobb, Jonathan. *The Hidden Injuries of Class.* London/Boston: Faber and Faber, 1993. First published in U.S.A. in 1972 by Alfred A. Knopf, New York, NY. p. 74.
"Results from the Michigan Panel Study of Income Dynamics suggest that the majority of these children will not escape poverty throughout their childhood, making the intergenerational transmission of poverty more likely" (Duncan, 1984, 1991). ("These" children refers to those "living in chronic material hardship.")	Pagani, Linda, Boulerice, Bernard, and Tremblay, Richard E. The Influence of Poverty on Children's Classroom Placement and Behavior Problems. Duncan, Greg J., and Brooks-Gunn, Jeanne, Editors. *Consequences of Growing Up Poor.* New York, NY: Russell Sage Foundation, 1997. p. 338.

There is a "high correlation between being a teenage remarried mother and a wide variety of indicators of low achievement (for example, failing to complete high school, being on welfare, being poor, and being out of the labor force)."

Haveman, Robert, Wolfe, Barbara, and Wilson, Kathryn. Childhood Poverty and Adolescent Schooling and Fertility Outcomes: Reduced-form and Structural Estimates. Duncan, Greg J., and Brooks-Gunn, Jeanne, Editors. *Consequences of Growing Up Poor.* New York, NY: Russell Sage Foundation, 1997. p. 421.

". . . [F]rom 1986 to 1992 the number of teen births in the United States increased from 472,000 to 518,000, an increase of nearly 50,000."

Ibid. pp. 421–422.

"While the majority of the teen births—about two-thirds—are to white teenagers, the proportion has been falling over time. By 1989, although African American women aged fifteen to nineteen composed 15.7 percent of this female age cohort, they accounted for 35 percent of the teen births. Indeed, teen births account for nearly one-quarter of all births to African American women."

Ibid. p. 422.

"Children born to unmarried teen mothers do not have an even start in life. They are more likely to grow up in a poor and mother-only family, live in a poor or under-class neighborhood, and experience high risks to both their health status and potential school achievement."

Ibid.

"Moreover, a relatively small percentage of teen unmarried mothers finish high school."

Ibid.

"Low achievement, grade repetition and classroom conduct problems are often precursors of school dropout, adolescent parenthood, joblessness and delinquency. The finding that poor children exhibit these problems at rates double those shown by non-poor children means the 'cycle of disadvantage' is still with us. Unless effective interventions are found and applied, many of these young people will go on to become adult non-workers and impoverished or dependent parents, possibly producing another generation of high-risk children."

Zill, Nicholaus. "The Changing Realities of Family Life." *Aspen Institute Quarterly.* Winter 1993. Volume 5. Number 1. p. 39.

Additive Model:
aha! Process's Approach to Building High-Achieving Schools

by Philip E. DeVol

The mission of aha! Process, Inc. is to positively impact the education and lives of individuals in poverty around the world. This mission is informed by the reality of life in poverty, research on the causes of poverty, and Dr. Ruby K. Payne's research and insights into economic diversity. The issues that aha! Process addresses are economic stability; the development of resources for individuals, families, and communities; and community sustainability. aha! Process provides an additive model that recognizes people in poverty, middle class, and wealth as problem solvers. The focus is on solutions, shared responsibilities, new insights, and interdependence. This work is about connectedness and relationships; it is about "us."

USING THE KNOWLEDGE OF PEOPLE IN POVERTY TO BUILD AN ACCURATE MENTAL MODEL OF POVERTY

Going directly to people in generational poverty, the people working the low-wage jobs, and listening to them talk about their concrete experiences is to learn from the experts, the people with the knowledge. The circle of life for a family at the bottom of the economic ladder is intense and stressful. Cars and public transportation are unreliable and insufficient, low-wage jobs come and go, housing is crowded and very costly, time and energy go into caring for the sick and trying to get health care, and many of the interactions with the dominant culture are demeaning and frustrating. For people in poverty, the arithmetic of life doesn't work. Housing costs are so high and wages so low that people have to double up, usually with family members, but often with people they may not know very well. All the elements in this mental model of poverty are interlocking: When the car won't start it sets off a chain reaction of missed appointments, being late to work, losing jobs, and searching for the next place to live. Vulnerability for people in poverty is concrete. When the price of gas goes to $2.20 a gallon it can mean having to work half a day to fill the tank. When one's attention is focused on the unfolding crisis of the day, people in poverty fall into what Paulo Freire calls the tyranny of the moment. Adds Peter Swartz: "The need to act overwhelms any willingness people have to learn." In this way poverty robs people of the their future stories and the commitment to education. It requires them to use reactive skills, not true choice making, to survive. And finally, it robs them of power; the power to solve problems in such a way as to change the environment—or to make future stories come true.

By continuing to listen, one learns that people survive these circumstances by developing relationships of mutual reliance and facing down problems with courage and humor. It is family, friends, and acquaintances who give you a place to stay, food to eat, a ride to work, and help with your children. It's not Triple A that you call when your car breaks down; it's Uncle Ray. People in poverty are the masters at making relationships quickly. Above all, they are problem solvers; they solve immediate, concrete problems all day long.

Unfortunately, the current operating mental model of our society appears to be that people in poverty are needy, deficient, diseased, and not to be trusted. Again, this can be learned by simply listening: listening to policymakers, commentators, and taxpayers who don't want their tax dollars to go to some- one who isn't trying, isn't motivated, is lazy, and so on. Another way to discover the underlying mental model is to observe its programs in action and work backwards. Three- to five-year lifetime limits for assistance, 90 days of services, work first . . . These policies point to frustration felt by those whose mental model of the poor is that they are needy, deficient, and diseased.

This inaccurate mental model is fed by media reports that favor soap operas to conceptual stories and individual stories to trends and the broader influences. The public hears about a fictitious "welfare queen" but not comprehensive studies. What is needed is a thorough understanding of the research on poverty.

STUDYING POVERTY RESEARCH TO FURTHER INFORM THE WORK OF AHA! PROCESS

David Shipler, author of *The Working Poor*, says that in the United States we are confused about the causes of poverty and, as a result, are confused about what to do about poverty (Shipler, 2004). In the interest of a quick analysis of the research on poverty, we have organized the studies into the following four clusters:

- Behaviors of the individual
- Human and social capital in the community
- Exploitation
- Political/economic structures

For the last four decades discourse on poverty has been dominated by proponents of two areas of research: those who hold that the *true* cause of poverty is the behaviors of individuals and those who hold that the *true* cause of poverty is political/economic structures. The first argues that if people in poverty would simply be punctual, sober, and motivated, poverty would be reduced if not eliminated. For them, the answer is individual initiative. Voter opinion tends to mirror the research. Forty percent of voters say that poverty is largely due to the lack of effort on the part of the individual (Bostrom, 2005). At the other end of the continuum, the argument is that globalization, as it is currently practiced, results in the loss of manufacturing jobs, forcing communities to attract business by offering the labor of their people at the lowest wages, thus creating a situation where a person can work full time and still be in poverty. In a virtual dead heat with the countering theory, 39 percent of voters think that poverty is largely due to circumstances beyond the individual's control. Unfortunately, both two sides tend to make either/or assertions as if to say, *It's either this or that—as if "this" is true and "that" is not.*

Either/or assertions have not served us well; it must be recognized that causes of poverty are a both/and reality. Poverty is caused by both the behaviors of the individual and political/economic structures—and everything in between. Definitions for the four clusters of research and sample topics are provided in the table on the next page.

Typically, communities put a great deal of effort into the first area of research: the behaviors of the individuals. "Work first" was one of the key themes of the welfare reform act of 1996. TANF (Temporary Assistance to Needy Families) organizations focused on getting people to work. The idea was that getting a job, any job, and learning to work were more important than going to job-training classes or receiving treatment. Community agencies offered treatment for substance abuse and mental-health problems, money-management classes, and programs to address literacy, teen pregnancies, language experience, and more. The mission of these agencies is not to work directly on poverty issues but to deal with co-existing problems. All of these agencies encourage their clients to change behaviors, recording and managing the changes through the use of plans and contracts, and often sanction clients who fail to adhere to treatment plans.

Community efforts to enhance human and social capital include the strategies found in Head Start, WIA programs, One-Stop centers, Earned Income Tax Credit, and other anti-poverty programs. In this area too, accountability and sanctions are used to measure and motivate community organizations. Schools that don't meet certain benchmarks are taken over by state departments; TANF organizations that don't meet certain benchmarks don't receive incentive funds. This isn't to make a blanket criticism of any of the programs that serve low-wage workers. In fact, many programs have great value to those who have used them. Rather, it's the almost exclusive focus on these two areas of research that is the problem.

Communities rarely develop strategies to restrict, replace, or sanction those who exploit people in poverty. Even those organizations charged with fighting poverty sometimes neglect this cause of poverty. In part, this comes

CAUSES OF POVERTY

1. Behaviors of the Individual

Definition: Research on the choices, behaviors, characteristics, and habits of people in poverty.

Sample topics:

Dependence on welfare	Racism and discrimination
Morality	Commitment to achievement
Crime	Spending habits
Single parenthood	Addiction, mental illness, domestic violence
Breakup of families	Planning skills
Intergenerational character traits	Orientation to the future
Work ethic	Language experience

2. Human and Social Capital in the Community

Definition: Research on the resources available to individuals, communities, and businesses.

Sample topics:

Intellectual capital	Childcare for working families
Social capital	Decline in neighborhoods
Availability of jobs	Decline in social morality
Availability of well-paying jobs	Urbanization
Racism and discrimination	Suburbanization of manufacturing
Availability and quality of education	Middle-class flight
Adequate skill sets	City and regional planning

3. Exploitation

Definition: Research on how people in poverty are exploited because they are in poverty.

Sample topics:

Drug trade	Gambling
Racism and discrimination	Temp work
Cash-advance lenders	Sweatshops
Sub-prime lenders	Sex trade
Lease-purchase outlets	Internet scams

4. Political/Economic Structures

Definition: Research on the economic, political, and social policies at the international, national, state, and local levels.

Sample topics:

Globalization	Taxation patterns
Corporate influence on legislators	Salary ratio of CEO to line worker
Declining middle class	Immigration patterns
De-industrialization	Economic disparity
Job loss	Racism and discrimination
Decline of unions	

from departmentalizing community services. People who work in organizations charged with serving those in poverty don't think of exploiters as their responsibility. That falls to law enforcement and policymakers.

Departmentalizing is even more pronounced when it comes to the causes of poverty that arise from political and economic structures. Community economic development is left to the market system, developers, businesses, corporations, the Chamber of Commerce, and elected officials. People who typically work with those in poverty don't see a role for themselves in the debate on economic development issues any more than those who are engaged in business ventures make a direct connection between their work and the well-being of people in poverty. And yet, in concrete terms, there is direct connection between quality of life and the actions of government and business. For the person in poverty it comes down to this: A person can get vocational training in a particular skill, get a job, and still be in poverty.

This all-too-common reality is the reason why communities must develop strategies across all four areas of research, not just the first two. To continue to focus exclusively on the first two areas of research is to invite more of the same—in short, more poverty. There is good research in all four areas; communities must develop strategies in all four areas if they are going to build resources and sustainability.

Alice O'Connor, author of *Poverty Knowledge*, says our society has typically looked at poverty through the prism of race and gender. She suggests that another analytic category is needed, that of economic class (O'Connor, 2001). In her seminal 1996 work *A Framework for Understanding Poverty*, Ruby Payne offered that prism. Since then aha! Process has published many books and produced many videos and workbooks that are used to address poverty across all four areas of research.

THE NEED FOR CHANGE: NAMING PROBLEMS AND FINDING SOLUTIONS

Any community or organization that sets out to address poverty, education, health care, justice, or community sustainability must acknowledge that it seeks change: change in the individual's behavior, change in community approaches, and/or change in political/economic structures. Put another way, there is no agency that receives money—be it federal, state, or private—to keep behaviors and conditions exactly as they are. We seek change because we perceive something to be wrong.

Naming the problem is the first step toward a solution, and the most important step, for if the problem is not named accurately the course of action based on that faulty assumption will only lead further and further from a solution. So naming problems accurately—making the correct diagnosis—is crucial because it is on those definitions that the theories of change and program activities are based.

But naming the problem isn't as simple as it seems. If a problem exists, is it due to something that is lacking, a shortage, a disadvantage, a handicap? It is here that planners, providers, and problem solvers tend to slide into what often is referred to as the deficit model. This model seems to derive from what William Miller calls the righting reflex. He says, "Human beings seem to have a built-in desire to set things right" (Miller, 2002). We see something that is wrong; we want to fix it. This tendency is all well and good as long as it's confined to one's own problems, but as soon as our fix-it intentions are focused on others, this approach quickly loses its charm and questions arise. Who is it that names the problem? Who is it a problem for? What evidence is provided? How broad or deep is the investigation? People from minority cultures and dominated groups are the first to ask these questions, for it is often their ways of raising children, their language uses, and their problem-solving strategies that are being labeled as having deficits by the mainstream culture. Nobody likes deficit labeling. So it is that the righting reflex leads to deficit models that few of us like—and even fewer defend, for good reasons.

There is no known father or mother of the deficit model. Nobody claims it, but the title or slur gets hung around the neck of those who use it, or appear to use it. Some people hold that James Coleman, who has been called the "father of busing," proposed a deficit model. A review of the body of his work would refute that label. His research on education, one of the largest research projects ever undertaken, discussed economic class and achievement in its complexities. It was legislators, businesspeople, school administrators, and others who were under pressure to "Fix it!" who simplified Coleman's work when they turned it into policy. There are two things to be learned from this. First, the deficit model is simplistic; it oversimplifies the research and applies the righting reflex. Second, there is research—and then there are those who use the research.

It's important to take a closer look at how problems get named and what the distinction is between naming problems and deficit labeling. The deficit model names the problem and blames the individual; the individual must change, whereas society can be left unaltered. It is, however, possible to name problems and not blame the individual. For example, Dr. James P. Comer, not by any stretch a proponent of the deficit model, does identify the family environment as crucial to a child's academic success. He points to hard science—brain research—that confirms the interactive process between the mediation (interpretation of reality) that children receive from caregivers before they come to school with the continuous mediation when children enter school. Quoting Comer: "Without [mediation] children can lose the 'sense'—the intelligence potential—they were born with. Children who have had positive developmental experiences before starting school acquire a set of beliefs, attitudes, and values—as well as social, verbal, and problem-solving skills, connections, and power—that they can use to succeed in school. They are the ones best able to elicit a positive response from people at school and bond with them." Read another way, this could appear as labeling low-income families with deficits. Of course, it isn't that because Comer acknowledges the problems that exist across the system; it's never as simple as the fault of a single person or group. The body of Comer's work reveals the true nature of his model (Comer, 2001).

Despite the fact that the deficit model seems to have no father or mother and is the work of policymakers more than researchers (and gets confused with the naming of problems), the deficit model is still for real. Its features are that it fixes the problems on the individual and therefore focuses on fixing the individual. Environmental conditions are translated into the characteristics of the individual and gradually turn into negative stereotypes. The talents, gifts, and skills of an individual get lost. In the deficit model the "glass is seen as half empty." The message becomes "you can't," and the impulse to care for and protect arises. Thus we have "special needs," "special programs," "special rooms," and "special personnel," all of which can lead to and foster dependency.

The lack of staff training can result in the deficit model appearing in the attitudes of the professionals, in individual bias, and inaccurate assumptions. Notes Comer: "Many successful people are inclined to attribute their situations to their own ability and effort—making them, in their minds, more deserving than less successful people. They ignore the support they received from families, networks of friends and kin, schools, and powerful others. They see no need for improved support of youth development" (Comer, 2001). Without training, staff members are likely to see deficits where there are none. A child who comes to school after getting up early to pump water from an outside well and whose mother hand-washes clothes once a week may be seen as dirty, less presentable, more lacking in physical resources than children who can shower in their own bathroom before coming to school and whose mother uses a washer and dryer. The first child has the resources and skills but isn't readily able to demonstrate those capabilities.

The lack of understanding on the part of the staff can lead to labeling that is hard to shake. If the school or agency doesn't provide some way for individuals to demonstrate their skills and resources, the glass will always appear to be half empty.

Problems are identified with student performance, drug use, teen pregnancy, inadequate skill sets, job retention, criminal behavior, poverty, and so on, all of which gives rise to fix-it programs. One Teacher Leaders Network online discussion participant offered this analogy about deficit-model programs: "We call it the 'chicken inspector' mindset. You see, the chicken inspector has been trained to look for something that isn't right, so that's his focus and that's what he finds—the things that are wrong. The more things he finds wrong, the better he feels he is doing his job."

The deficit model finds its way into the design of programs. Legislators and professionals set policy and create departments and programs. Each department is expected to fix the piece of the pie that falls under its purview. These reactions to the latest problem set up a random approach to problem solving and result in remedial programs focused on the behaviors of the individual while losing sight of the whole system made up of families, neighborhoods, communities, and sociopolitical/economic structures.

This isn't to suggest that policymakers and program designers set out to apply the deficit model. It's more likely that they select some other approach but for any number of reasons fail to adhere to their espoused theory (what is said) and slide into a "theory of use" (what is done) that resembles the deficit model (Senge, 1994). Perhaps the most common reason for this slip is that it's easier to describe, plan for, monitor, and sanction the behaviors of individuals than it is to hold organizations, communities, and systems accountable in the same way (Washburne, 1958). The fact is that the deficit model is resilient, and we slide back into it easily.

Opposite the deficit model are many models that offer what the deficit model does not. They go by many names: positive model, developmental assets, competency, value-based, and strength-based . . . to name a few. Other models have been assigned names by their developers: Health Realization, Resiliency in Action, Comer Model, and Motivational Interviewing to name but four. Each of these models has its distinct theory and practices, but the one thing they have in common is that they see "the glass as half full."

Positive models too are not without their critics. For example, child-protection workers point out that reframing the behaviors and characteristics of victims of abuse into strengths is naïve. No matter how resilient the child, the fact remains that the child has very little control over his/her environment and the behaviors of adults. Educators note that children in poverty have been exposed to more in their few years than many adults. In some ways they seem to have adult capabilities; they take care of themselves and feel confident they can handle big decisions. But the educators caution against accepting this claim. According to a recent piece by Craig Sautter, "We as adults need to remember that they are not adults. They still have a lot of growing and developing to do and still need the guidance of adults who can be there to help them through their growing-up period" (Sautter, 2005).

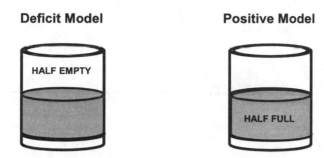

The additive model, a term used by Ruby Payne to describe the work of her company, aha! Process, combines the value of accurate problem identification with a positive, strength-based, communitywide approach to change. Applying the glass half empty/half full model to the three economic classes and the work of aha! Process would look like this:

For the Person in Poverty

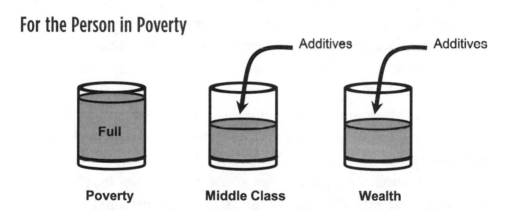

To survive in poverty, individuals must have reactive, sensory, and non-verbal skills. This means they have the ability to read situations, establish relationships, and solve immediate and concrete problems quickly. In that environment, individuals have a full glass; they have the assets and strengths to survive.

When individuals in poverty encounter the middle-class world of work, school, and other institutions, they do not have all the assets necessary to survive in that environment because what is needed there are proactive, abstract, and verbal skills. The additive model offers insight into how hidden rules of economic class work, along with a framework for building resources, a way to fill up the glass.

When the person in middle class encounters wealth, the same is true—but to a greater extent.

For the Person in Middle Class

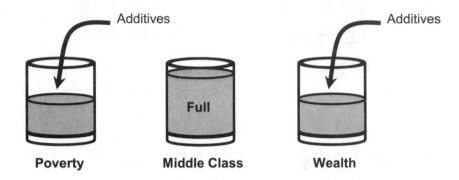

Individuals raised in a middle-class environment learn the hidden rules, mindsets, and means of survival the same way persons in poverty or wealth do: through osmosis. To learn the survival rules of one's environment, virtually all one has to do is breathe. So the glass is full so long as individuals remain in their environment. But should those persons suddenly find themselves in poverty—or even in a poverty neighborhood—would they have the assets needed to survive there? The glass would be half empty. But there is a more common scenario that brings people in middle class and people in poverty together; that is in the institutions run by middle-class people. In this scenario both groups come with a glass half full because they may not understand the rules or value the assets of the other person or the other class. Here is where the additive model can help. It names the problem and offers insight and awareness; it opens the way to build relationships and eventually to better outcomes for both.

As middle-class individuals interact with people in wealth they may not know any more about the rules of survival in wealth than the person in poverty knows about the rules of middle class (and how the values of the additive model apply).

The additive model has something to offer people in wealth as well.

For the Person in Wealth

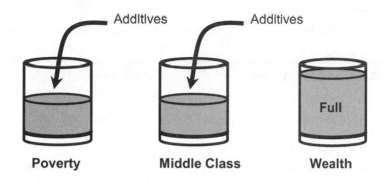

Where the worlds of wealth, middle class, and poverty intersect, the additive model can assist. Due to their connections, influence, and power, people in wealth often are in the position to design the policies and directions of the institutions that the middle class run and that the people in poverty use. If wealthy individuals' poverty and middle-class glass is only half full and all they know is their own rules of survival, then it can result in policies that are ineffective and counterproductive.

To better understand the additive model, we must consider aha! Process definitions and core concepts.

RESOURCES

Resources: The following resources are quality-of-life indicators that are described in almost all aha! Process publications.

- Financial
- Emotional
- Mental
- Spiritual
- Physical
- Support systems
- Relationships/role models
- Knowledge of hidden rules

Poverty: the extent to which an individual or community does without these resources.

Prosperity/sustainability: the extent to which an individual or community has these resources.

By these definitions it is easy to see that an individual may have low financial resources and at the same time have other resources that are very high. Of course, the opposite is true too: One can have high financial resources and be impoverished in other ways.

This approach emphasizes that every individual's story is different and takes into account the culture in which one lives. And yet, as a general rule, the additive model holds that to have high resources is better than to not have high resources. It's preferable to have financial stability than to be unable to pay for basic needs. It's preferable to have many positive relationships than to live in isolation. It's preferable to be able to identify feelings, choose behaviors, and get along with others than to be emotionally destructive.

The additive model holds that:

- Resources are to be developed by communities, families, and individuals. In fact, it is the appropriate role, or "job" if you will, of individuals, families, and communities to grow resources for oneself, one's family, and the community.

- The optimal way to build resources is to build on one's strengths. Focusing on low resources, weaknesses, and what is absent not only is no fun, it simply isn't effective.

- We must develop resource-building strategies across all four areas of poverty research. The deficit model is at work when a community focuses its anti-poverty strategies on the behaviors of the individual.

Ruby Payne's research on the hidden rules of economic class is another key component of the aha! Process approach. It is this analytic category that provides a new lens through which to examine poverty and prosperity issues. Again, some definitions will help clarify the additive model.

HIDDEN RULES OF ECONOMIC CLASS

Hidden rules: the unspoken cues and habits of a group. All groups have hidden rules; you know you belong when you don't have to explain anything you say or do. These rules are held by racial, ethnic, religious, regional, and cultural groups . . . to name a few. An individual's cultural fabric is made up of many threads, one of which is economic class. Where the threads are woven together the different cultures act on behaviors of the individual and group. Of these rules, economic class is a surprisingly strong thread, one that is often overlooked—or at least minimized.

The additive model holds that:

■ The hidden rules arise from the environment in which a person lives, that they help persons survive in the class in which they were raised. This means that the rules of class are not to be criticized, but that we simply add options, new rules, a wider range of responses, an ability to negotiate more environments. While these are framed as choices and not identity, any individuals who begin to work on achievements—such as economic stability, education, or getting sober—are changing their identity. How they make the transition is a choice: Will they stay connected with people from their past, or will they move into new circles? This is an individual and often painful choice/process. Being aware of the choice can smooth the process, whatever the decision.

■ It is beneficial for middle-class people to learn the hidden rules of poverty—and not just so they're able to help people in poverty make changes, but because the hidden rules of poverty have value in their own right. Perhaps first among these is the value of relationships and the time given to them. The ability people in poverty have to establish quick but intimate relationships is an asset. In the additive model, change takes place, not just in the individual but in the theories of change and program designs of organizations. Middle-class organizations often have based their work on middle-class mindsets without an adequate mental model of poverty or knowledge of the hidden rules of the people they serve.

It is by adding to the hidden rules that one is raised with that people develop a range of responses that will give them control over their situations and open doors to new opportunities.

LANGUAGE ISSUES

The aha! Process approach calls for an extensive discussion of language issues, including definitions of the registers of language, discourse patterns, story structures, language experience in the first three years of life, cognitive issues, and strategies to deal with all of these. As a body of work, aha! Process's many books, workbooks, videos, classroom strategies, program design strategies together make up a remarkable representation of the additive model. It is here that the model calls for an accurate naming of problems where the word deficit is used.

The additive model holds that:

- People build relationships by using the registers of language and discourse patterns skillfully.

- The strengths and uses of each register are encouraged where they can be most skillfully applied.

- Classroom interventions and agency strategies must be based on a clear understanding of the issues and a clear definition of the problems.

- The interventions themselves are built on the assets of the individual and the necessary changes fall as much on the professionals as on the individuals in poverty.

- Learning structures in the brain can be enhanced, but only by knowing the exact nature of the thinking that is occurring. In school settings the intervention cannot be random or general. The strategies offered by aha! Process are grade- and subject-specific.

■ A rich language experience benefits children and prepares them for the world of work and school.

■ Teachers value the language experience that children bring with them to school and prepare students to be able to skillfully navigate a wide range of language situations.

■ In social service settings with adults, the additive model calls for the staff to become bilingual (able to translate from formal register to casual register).

■ Change messages—be they about cardiovascular disease, breast feeding, birth weight, or the prevention of drug use—often taught in the formal register are now taught through a self-discovery process and by using mental models. Communication is meaningful and not just what Robert Sapolsky calls middle-class noise (Sapolsky, 1998).

FAMILY STRUCTURE

Matriarchal structure: All families have capabilities and strengths, and all families are faced with demands. In the course of life all families must face suffering and hard times, but some families seem to have more than their share of suffering to contend with. Under ordinary demands and stressors, families will become stronger as a result of their struggles. But there are some things that can overrun and overwhelm a family's capabilities; those include chronic addiction, mental illness, physical illness, and poverty (Henderson, 1996). People in poverty sometimes contend with more than poverty alone, and poverty itself is so stressful that there is a direct correlation between poverty and stress-related illnesses (Sapolsky, 1998). In high-demand conditions, families take on a structure that fits the survival needs of the family. In that context, the matriarchal structure and associated patterns of behavior are assets, but if viewed in light of a deficit model are often seen as negative or even as lacking in morals. A matriarchal family is not synonymous with a dysfunctional family. As in all economic classes, dysfunctional things may happen, but living in poverty does not equate with dysfunctional behaviors. The additive model provides an understanding and appreciation of matriarchal families and offers new information and ways of increasing resources.

The additive model holds that:

- Family structures evolve to meet the survival needs of the family and that they are strengths.

- As with aha! Process knowledge, awareness gives people optional ways to stabilize the chaotic circle of life, to envision new patterns and stories, to practice choice, and to build new resources.

SHARING AHA! PROCESS KNOWLEDGE WITH ADULTS IN POVERTY

Co-investigation: Sharing aha! Process knowledge with people in poverty is done through a group investigation of the causes of poverty, examining the impact of poverty on the individual, and exploring new information. Individuals in the group assess their own resources and make plans to build their own future story. Here's one way of articulating the challenges faced by people in poverty:

Poverty traps people in the tyranny of the moment, making it very difficult to attend to abstract information or plan for the future (Freire, 1999; Sharron, 1996; Galeano, 1998)—*the very things needed to build resources and financial assets. There are many causes of poverty, some having to do with the choices of the poor, but at least as many stemming from community conditions and political/economic structures* (O'Connor, 2001; Brouwer, 1998; Gans, 1995).

The additive model holds that:

- People in poverty need an accurate perception of how poverty impacts them and an understanding of economic realities as a starting point both for reasoning and for developing plans for transition (Freire, 1999; Galeano, 1998).

- Using mental models for learning and reasoning, people can move from the concrete to the abstract (Freedman, 1996; Harrison, 2000; Sharron, 1996; Mattaini 1993; Jaworski, 1996; Senge, 1994).

- People can be trusted to make good use of accurate information, presented in a meaningful way by facilitators who provide a relationship of mutual respect and act as co-investigators (Freire, 1999; Sapolsky, 1998; McKnight, 1995; Pransky, 1998; Farson, 1997).

- Using Ruby Payne's definition of the resources necessary for a full life, as well as her insights into the hidden rules of economic class, people can evaluate themselves and their situation, choose behaviors, and make plans to build resources (Miller, 2002).

- The community must provide services, support, and meaningful opportunities during transition and over the long term (Putnam, 2002; Kretzmann, 1993).

- In partnership with people from middle class and wealth, individuals in poverty can solve community and systemic problems that contribute to poverty (Phillips, 2002; Kretzmann, 1993).

AHA! PROCESS KNOWLEDGE AND COMMUNITY SUSTAINABILITY

Community sustainability: This is an issue that all communities, states, and nations must now face. The world has seen several revolutionary changes: the change from hunter/gatherer societies to agriculture, the industrial revolution, the information age, and now the era in which we must determine how to use our resources and live in our environment—and yet retain vital resources for our children and grandchildren.

The mission of aha! Process—to directly impact the education and lives of individuals in poverty around the world—leads to a role in this revolution. Communities are awakening to the reality that they do not offer a sustainable way of life to their children and are looking for direction. Equity and critical mass impact the changes that are taking place. If a community allows any group to be disenfranchised for any reason (religion, race, class), the entire community becomes economically poorer (Sowell, 1998). When poverty reaches the point of critical mass in a community and efforts to reverse the problem don't succeed, the people with the most resources tend to move out of the community, leaving behind enclaves of poverty. At this point the community is no longer sustainable.

Responding to the impending crisis with the mindset that created it and with the strategies that have been used to address poverty to date is to invite more of the same results: more poverty and more communities at risk.

aha! Process defines community as any group that has something in common and the potential for acting together (Taylor-Ide 2002). The rich social capital that peaked in the post–World War II era—and that has been on the decline since—must be restored (Putnam, 2000). The barn-raising metaphor for communities where citizens contribute to the building of the barn with their particular skills, gifts, and talents must replace the vending-machine metaphor, which is currently in use. The vending-machine metaphor reduces community members to consumers or shoppers who put 75 cents into the machine expecting 75 cents of goods and services in return. With that mindset, it's no surprise that we find people kicking, shaking, and cursing the vending machine.

The additive model holds that:

- It's better to be a barn raiser than a consumer.

- All three classes must be at the table.

- Communities must have a shared understanding and a common vocabulary to build critical mass that is willing and motivated to make the necessary changes.

- Strategies must cover all the causes of poverty—from the behaviors of individuals to political/economic structures.

- Communities must build intellectual capital.

- Long-term plans of 20 to 25 years are needed.

- Quality-of-life indicators must be monitored and reported regularly in the same way that economic indicators are monitored and reported.

CONCLUSION

aha! Process offers a unique understanding of economic diversity that can give individuals, families, and communities new ways of solving problems. It is the hope of aha! Process that 100 years from now poverty will no longer be viewed as economically inevitable. Two hundred years ago slavery was thought to be an economic necessity. It was not. One hundred fifty years ago it was believed that women were not capable of voting. That also was not true. We fervently hope that by 2100 individuals and society at large will no longer believe that poverty is inevitable. It is only by applying an additive model that we will understand and address both poverty and the underlying factors that have perpetuated it.

WORKS CITED

Andreas, Steve, & Faulkner, Charles. (Eds.) (1994). *NLP: The New Technology of Achievement*. New York, NY: Quill.

Bostrom, Meg. (2005). Together for Success: Communicating Low-Wage Work as Economy, Not Poverty. Ford Foundation Project. Douglas Gould & Co.

Brouwer, Steve. (1998). *Sharing the Pie: A Citizen's Guide to Wealth and Power in America*. New York, NY: Henry Holt & Company.

Comer, James P. (2001). Schools That Develop Children. *The American Prospect*. Volume 12. Number 7. April 23.

DeVol, Philip E. (2004). *Getting Ahead in a Just-Gettin'-by World: Building Your Resources for a Better Life.* Highlands, TX: aha! Process.

Farson, Richard. (1997). *Management of the Absurd: Paradoxes in Leadership.* New York, NY: Touchstone.

Freedman, Jill, & Combs, Gene. (1996). *Narrative Therapy: The Social Construction of Preferred Realities.* New York, NY: W.W. Norton & Company.

Freire, Paulo. (1999). *Pedagogy of the Oppressed.* New York, NY: Continuum Publishing Company.

Fussell, Paul. (1983). *Class: A Guide Through the American Status System.* New York, NY: Touchstone.

Galeano, Eduardo. (1998). *Upside Down: A Primer for the Looking-Glass World.* New York, NY: Metropolitan Books.

Gans, Herbert J. (1995). *The War Against the Poor.* New York, NY: Basic Books.

Harrison, Lawrence E., & Huntington, Samuel P. (Eds.). (2000). *Culture Matters: How Values Shape Human Progress.* New York, NY: Basic Books.

Henderson, Nan. (1996). *Resiliency in Schools: Making It Happen for Students and Educators.* Thousand Oaks, CA: Corwin Press.

Jaworski, Joseph. (1996). *Synchronicity: The Inner Path of Leadership.* San Francisco, CA: Berrett-Koehler Publishers.

Kahlenberg, Richard, D. (2001). Learning from James Coleman. *Public Interest.* Summer.

Kretzmann, John, & McKnight, John. (1993). *Building Communities From the Inside Out: A Path Toward Finding and Mobilizing a Community's Assets.* Chicago, IL: ACTA Publications.

Lewis, Oscar. (1966). The Culture of Poverty. *Scientific American.* Volume 215. Number 4. pp. 19–25.

Mattaini, Mark A. (1993). *More Than a Thousand Words: Graphics for Clinical Practice.* Washington, DC: NASW Press.

McKnight, John. (1995). *The Careless Society: Community and Its Counterfeits.* New York, NY: Basic Books.

Miller, William R., & Rollnick, Stephen. (2002). *Motivational Interviewing: Preparing People for Change*, Second Edition. New York, NY: Guilford Press.

O'Connor, Alice. (2001). *Poverty Knowledge: Social Science, Social Policy, and the Poor in Twentieth-Century U.S. History.* Princeton, NJ: Princeton University Press.

Payne, Ruby K., DeVol, Philip, & Dreussi Smith, Terie. (2001). *Bridges Out of Poverty: Strategies for Professionals and Communities.* Highlands, TX: aha! Process.

Phillips, Kevin. (2002). *Wealth and Democracy: A Political History of the American Rich.* New York, NY: Broadway Books.

Pransky, Jack. (1998). *Modello: A Story of Hope for the Inner-City and Beyond.* Cabot, VT: NEHRI Publications.

Putnam, Robert D. (2000). *Bowling Alone: The Collapse and Revival of American Community.* New York, NY: Simon & Schuster.

Sapolsky, Robert M. (1998). *Why Zebras Don't Get Ulcers: An Updated Guide to Stress, Stress-Related Diseases, and Coping.* New York, NY: W.H. Freeman & Company.

Sautter, Craig. (2005). Who Are Today's City Kids? Beyond the "Deficit Model." North Central Regional Educational Laboratory, a subsidiary of Learning Points Associates. http://www.ncrel.org/sdrs/cityschl/city1_1a.htm

Senge, Peter M. (1994). *The Fifth Discipline: The Art & Practice of The Learning Organization.* New York, NY: Currency Doubleday.

Sharron, Howard, & Coulter, Martha. (1996). *Changing Children's Minds: Feuerstein's Revolution in the Teaching of Intelligence.* Birmingham, England: Imaginative Minds.

Shipler, David K. (2004). *The Working Poor: Invisible in America.* New York, NY: Alfred A. Knopf.

Sowell, Thomas. (1998). Race, Culture and Equality. *Forbes*. October 5.

Sowell, Thomas. (1997). *Migrations and Cultures: A World View*. New York, NY: HarperCollins.

Taylor-Ide, Daniel, & Taylor, Carl, E. (2002). *Just and Lasting Change: When Communities Own Their Futures*. Baltimore, MD: Johns Hopkins University Press.

Washburne, Chandler. (1958). Conflicts Between Educational Theory and Structure. *Educational Theory*. Volume 8. Number 2. April.

Bibliography

Anderson, Judith, Hollinger, Debra, & Conaty, Joseph. (1993). Re-examining the Relationship Between School Poverty and Student Achievement. *ERS Spectrum.* Spring. pp. 21–31.

Bandler, Richard, & Grinder, John. (1979). *Frogs into Princes.* Moab, UT: Real People Press.

Barnitz, John G. (1994). Discourse Diversity: Principles for Authentic Talk and Literacy Instruction. *Classroom Talk about Text: What Teenagers and Teachers Come to Know about the World through Talk about Text.* Rosalind Horowitz. (Ed.). International Reading Association publication.

Berliner, D.C. (1988). *Implications of Studies of Expertise in Pedagogy for Teacher Education and Evaluation.* Paper presented at 1988 Educational Testing Service Invitational Conference on New Directions for Teacher Assessment. New York, NY.

Berne, Eric. (1996). *Games People Play: The Basic Handbook of Transactional Analysis.* New York, NY: Ballantine Books.

Bianchi, Suzanne M. (1990). America's Children: Mixed Prospects. *Population Bulletin.* Volume 45. Number 1. June.

Bloom, Benjamin. (1976). *Human Characteristics and School Learning.* New York, NY: McGraw-Hill Book Company.

Boals, Beverly M., et al. (1990). *Children in Poverty: Providing and Promoting a Quality Education.* ERIC document.

Bradshaw, John. (1988). *Bradshaw on: The Family.* Deerfield Beach, FL: Health Communications.

Caine, Renate Nummela, & Caine, Geoffrey. (1991). *Making Connections: Teaching and the Human Brain*. Alexandria, VA: Association of Supervision and Curriculum Development.

Capponi, Pat. (1997). *Dispatches from the Poverty Line*. Toronto, Ontario, Canada: Penguin Books.

Collins, Bryn C. (1997). *Emotional Unavailability: Recognizing It, Understanding It, and Avoiding Its Trap*. Lincolnwood, IL: NTC/Contemporary Publishing Company.

Comer, James. (1995). Lecture given at Education Service Center, Region IV. Houston, TX.

Connell, R.W. (1994). *Poverty and Education*. Harvard Educational Review. Volume 64. Number 2. Summer.

Cook, John T., & Brown, Larry J. (1993). *Two Americas: Racial Differences in Child Poverty in the U.S.: A Linear Trend Analysis to the Year 2010*. Research-in-progress working paper. Medford, MA: Tufts University.

Coontz, Stephanie. (1995). The American Family and the Nostalgia Trap. *Phi Delta Kappan*. Volume 76. Number 7. March.

Covey, Stephen R. (1989). *The Seven Habits of Highly Effective People: Powerful Lessons in Personal Change*. New York, NY: Simon & Schuster.

Duncan, Greg J., & Brooks-Gunn, Jeanne. (Eds.). (1997). *Consequences of Growing Up Poor*. New York, NY: Russell Sage Foundation.

Edelman, Peter B., & Ladner, Joyce. (Eds.). (1991). *Adolescence and Poverty: Challenge for the 1990s*. Washington, DC: Center for National Policy.

Educational Attainments of Students Living in Poverty. Report of the Department of Education to the Governor and the General Assembly of Virginia. Senate Document Number 13. (1993). Richmond, VA: Virginia State Department of Education.

Einbinder, Susan D. (1993). *Five Million Children: 1993 Update*. New York, NY: National Center for Children in Poverty, Columbia University.

Eitzen, Stanley D. (1992). Problem Students: The Sociocultural Roots. *Phi Delta Kappan.* April.

Feuerstein, Reuven, et al. (1980). *Instrumental Enrichment: An Intervention Program for Cognitive Modifiability.* Glenview, IL: Scott, Foresman & Co.

Forward, Susan, with Frazier, Donna. (n.d.). *Emotional Blackmail.* New York, NY: HarperCollins Publishers.

Fox, Steven. (1997). The Controversy over Ebonics. *Phi Delta Kappan.* Volume 79. Number 3. November.

Fussel, Paul. (1983). *Class.* New York, NY: Ballantine Books.

Gardner, Howard. (1991). *The Unschooled Mind: How Children Think and How Schools Should Teach.* New York, NY: Basic Books.

Garmezy, Norman. (1991). Resiliency and Vulnerability to Adverse Developmental Outcomes Associated with Poverty. *American Behavioral Scientist.* Volume 34. Number 4. March-April. pp. 416–430.

Gee, James Paul. (1987). What Is Literacy? *Teaching and Learning: The Journal of Natural Inquiry.* Volume 2. Number 1. Fall.

Goleman, Daniel. (1995). *Emotional Intelligence.* New York, NY: Bantam Books.

Haberman, Martin. (1995). *Star Teachers of Children in Poverty.* Madison, WI: Phi Delta Kappa.

Harrington, Michael. (1962). *The Other America.* New York, NY: Simon & Schuster.

Harris, Lorwen, Connie. (1988). Facts about Texas Children. Excerpted from *Children, Choice, and Change.* Austin, TX: Hogg Foundation for Mental Health, Texas University.

Hodgkinson, Harold L. (1995). What Should We Call People? Race, Class, and the Census for 2000. *Phi Delta Kappan.* October.

Immigrant Children in the United States are Growing in Number and Facing Substantial Economic Hardship. (2002). New York, NY: National Center for Children in Poverty, Columbia University.

Idol, Lorna, & Jones, B.F. (Eds.). (1991). *Educational Values and Cognitive Instruction: Implications for Reform.* Hillsdale, NJ: Lawrence Erlbaum Associates.

Jones, B.F., Pierce, J., & Hunter, B. (1988). Teaching students to construct graphic representations. *Educational Leadership.* Volume 46. Number 4. pp. 20–25.

Joos, Martin. (1967). The Styles of the Five Clocks. *Language and Cultural Diversity in American Education.* 1972. Abrahams, R.D., & Troike, R.C. (Eds.). Englewood Cliffs, NJ: Prentice-Hall.

Kaplan, R.B. (1984). Cultural Thought Patterns in Intercultural Education. In McKay, S. (Ed.). (1984). *Composing in a Second Language.* Rowley, MA: Newbury House Publishers. pp. 43–62.

Knapp, Michael S., et al. (1993). *Academic Challenge for the Children of Poverty. Study of Academic Instruction for Disadvantaged Students. Volume 1: Findings and Conclusions.* Washington, DC: Policy Studies Associates.

Knapp, Michael S., & Shields, Patrick M. (1990). Reconceiving Academic Instruction for the Children of Poverty. *Phi Delta Kappan.* June.

Knapp, Michael S., & Shields, Patrick M. (Eds.). (1991). *Better Schooling for the Children of Poverty: Alternatives to Conventional Wisdom.* Berkeley, CA: McCutchan Publishing Corporation.

Kozol, Jonathan. (1991). *Savage Inequalities.* New York, NY: HarperPerennial.

Kozol, Jonathan. (1995). *Amazing Grace.* New York, NY: Crown Publishers.

Laborde, Genie Z. (1983). *Influencing with Integrity: Management Skills for Communication and Negotiation.* Palo Alto, CA: Syntony Publishing.

Language Barriers Are More Complex Than We Might Think. (1992). *CSBA News*. Sacramento, CA: California School Boards Association. Volume 4. Number 9. November.

Larson, Jackie. (1993). Maria Montano-Harmon: A Call for Heightened Awareness. *Texas Lone Star*. November.

Lewis, Anne C. (1996). Breaking the Cycle of Poverty. *Phi Delta Kappan*. Volume 78. Number 3. November.

Lewis, Oscar. (1971). The Culture of Poverty. Penchef, Esther. (Ed.). *Four Horsemen: Pollution, Poverty, Famine, Violence*. San Francisco, CA: Canfield Press.

Lewit, Eugene M. (1993). Child Indicators: Children in Poverty. *Future-of-Children*. Volume 3. Number 1. Spring.

Lewit, Eugene M. (1993). Why Is Poverty Increasing Among Children? *Future-of-Children*. Volume 3. Number 2. Summer/Fall.

Making Schools Work for Children in Poverty: A New Framework Prepared by the Commission on Chapter 1. (1992). Washington, DC: American Association of School Administrators. December.

Marzano, Robert J., & Arredondo, Daisy. (1986). *Tactics for Thinking*. Aurora, CO: Mid Continent Regional Educational Laboratory.

Mayer, Susan E. (1997). *What Money Can't Buy*. Cambridge, MA: Harvard University Press.

Mills, C. Wright. (1956). *The Power Elite*. New York, NY: Oxford University Press.

Miranda, Leticia C. (1991). *Latino Child Poverty in the United States*. Washington, DC: Children's Defense Fund.

Montano-Harmon, Maria Rosario. (1991). Discourse Features of Written Mexican Spanish: Current Research in Contrastive Rhetoric and Its Implications. *Hispania*. Volume 74. Number 2. May. pp. 417–425.

Moynihan, Daniel Patrick. (1989). Welfare Reform: Serving America's Children. *Teachers College Record.* Volume 90. Number 3. Spring.

Natale, Jo Anna. (1992). Growing Up the Hard Way. *American School Board Journal.* October. pp. 20–27.

Natriello, Gary, McGill, Edward L., & Pallas, Aaron M. (1990). *Schooling Disadvantaged Children: Racing Against Catastrophe.* New York, NY: Teachers College Press, Columbia University.

O'Neill, John. (1991). A Generation Adrift? *Educational Leadership.* September. pp. 4–10.

Palincsar, A.S., & Brown, A.L. (1984). The reciprocal teaching of comprehension-fostering and comprehension-monitoring activities. *Cognition and Instruction.* Volume 1. Number 2. pp. 117–175.

Penchef, Esther. (Ed.). (1971). *Four Horsemen: Pollution, Poverty, Famine, Violence.* San Francisco, CA: Canfield Press.

Renchler, Ron. (1993). Poverty and Learning. *ERIC Digest.* Number 83. Eugene, OR: ERIC Clearinghouse on Educational Management.

Rodriguez, Luis J. (1993). *Always Running.* New York, NY: Simon & Schuster.

Rural Children: Increasing Poverty Rates Pose Educational Challenges. Briefing Report to the Chairwoman, Congressional Rural Caucus, House of Representatives. (1994). Washington, DC: General Accounting Office.

Samuelson, Robert J. (1997). The Culture of Poverty. *Newsweek.* Volume 129. Number 18. May 5.

School Age Demographics: Recent Trends Pose New Educational Challenges. Briefing Report to Congressional Requesters. (1993). Washington, DC: General Accounting Office.

Sennett, Richard, & Cobb, Jonathan. (1993). *The Hidden Injuries of Class.* London/Boston: Faber & Faber. First published in U.S.A. in 1972 by Alfred A. Knopf, New York, NY.

Shapiro, Joseph P., Friedman, Dorian, Meyer, Michelle, & Loftus, Margaret. (1996). Invincible Kids. *U.S. News & World Report*. Volume 121. Number 19. November 11.

Sharron, Howard, & Coulter, Martha. (1994). *Changing Children's Minds: Feuerstein's Revolution in the Teaching of Intelligence*. Exeter, Great Britain: BPC Wheatons Ltd.

Stern, Mark J. (1987). The Welfare of Families. *Educational Leadership*. March. pp. 82–87.

Takeuchi, David T., et al. (1991). Economic Stress in the Family and Children's Emotional and Behavioral Problems. *Journal of Marriage and the Family*. Volume 53. Number 4. November. pp. 1031–1041.

Texas School Improvement Initiative: Peer Evaluator Training Manual. (1995). Austin, TX: Texas Education Agency.

The Poorest Among Us. (1996). *U.S. News & World Report*. Volume 121. Number 25. December 23.

Thornburg, Kathy R., Hoffman, Stevie, Remeika, Corinne. (1991). Youth at Risk: Society at Risk. *Elementary School Journal*. Volume 91. Number 3. January. pp. 199–208.

Vobejda, Barbara. (1994). Half of Nation's Kids Not in "Typical" Family. *Houston Chronicle*. August 30.

Wake Up America: Columbia University Study Shatters Stereotypes of Young Child Poverty. (1996). Website: http://cpmcnet.columbia.edu/news/press_releases/12-11-96.html. December 11.

Wheatley, Margaret J. (1992). *Leadership and the New Science*. San Francisco, CA: Berrett-Koehler Publishers.

Woodard, Samuel L. (1992). Academic Excellence in the Urban Environment: Overcoming the Odds. *NAASP* (National Association of Secondary School Principals) Bulletin. Volume 76. Number 546. October. pp. 57–61.

Zill, Nicholaus. (1993). The Changing Realities of Family Life. *Aspen Institute Quarterly*. Volume 5. Number 1. Winter. pp. 27–51.

Index

Eye-openers at ...
www.ahaprocess.com

- If you are interested in more information regarding seminars or training for *A Framework for Understanding Poverty* including long-term Technical Assistance for Schools, we invite you to our Website, www.ahaprocess.com.

- There you also can join our *aha!* News List. Receive the latest income and poverty statistics *free* when you join! Then periodic news and updates will follow.

- Additional programs/DVD series offered by aha! Process include:

  New! DVD *Boys in Crisis—Why It Matters and What You Can Do About It*

  aha! Classroom Discipline SIMulation—Grades K–2, 3–5, 6–8, and 9–12 (download a free demo of the software from our website). Software purchase includes free *Discipline Strategies for the Classroom* book.

  Meeting Standards & Raising Test Scores—When You Don't Have Much Time or Money (DVD and manual)

  Bridges Out of Poverty: Strategies for Professionals and Communities (7 DVDs)

  Tucker Signing Strategies for Reading (DVD and training manual)

  Reading by Age 5 (DVD and book)

- For a complete listing of products, please visit www.ahaprocess.com.

Order Form

Please send me _____ copy/copies of *A Framework for Understanding Poverty.*

Enclosed is payment for:

Books $ _____

Shipping $ _____

Subtotal $ _____

Sales tax $ _____
(only residents of Alabama, Florida, Georgia, Kentucky,
Nebraska, New Mexico, Tennessee, and Texas)

Total $ _____

> **1–4 BOOKS:**
> $22.00/each + $4.50 first book plus
> $2.00 each additional book
>   shipping/handling
>
> **5 OR MORE BOOKS:**
> $15.00/each + 8% shipping/handling

UPS Ship-to Address (no post office boxes, please)

Name _____

Organization _____

Address _____

_____

Phone _____

E-mail _____

Method of Payment

PO # _____

Credit card type_____ Exp. _____

Credit card # _____

Check $ _____ Check # _____

Thanks for your order!

Process, Inc.
www.ahaprocess.com

PO Box 727 • Highlands, TX 77562-0727
(800) 424-9484 • fax (281) 426-5600

Ruby Payne's New Book Offers Strategies That Work

NEW Under-Resourced Learners:
**8 Strategies to Boost Student
Achievement**
by Ruby K. Payne, Ph.D.

Millions of school-age children are "under-resourced" and at risk of failure in school. This book identifies resources all students need and delivers proven, practical strategies for building up these resources for every student in the school. Determine best strategies and interventions—and develop strategies for building relationships and increasing family support systems. Monitor progress and adjust strategies for student success.

Inside, you'll find:

- Strategies for developing relational learning
- Tools for identifying procedures to reduce discipline referrals
- Six-step process for following each student's performance—and addressing AYP
- Checklists for assessing resources of students
- Strategies for working effectively with parents

Today's classroom teachers are desperate for a way to reach so many disengaged, floundering students; this book is the answer. I found this book gave me additional strategies that I can use in my classroom immediately.

– Marye Jane Brockinton
Fifth- and Sixth-Grades Teacher Cabot, AR
